FOR SUCH A TIME AS

This

MY FAITH JOURNEY THROUGH THE WHITE HOUSE AND BEYOND

KAYLEIGH MCENANY

Liberatio
Protocol

A LIBERATIO PROTOCOL BOOK
An Imprint of Post Hill Press

For Such a Time as This:
My Faith Journey through the White House and Beyond
© 2021 by Kayleigh McEnany
All Rights Reserved

ISBN: 978-1-63758-235-0
ISBN (eBook): 978-1-63758-236-7

Cover photo by Bryan Manicchia
Cover design by Cody Corcoran

This is a work of nonfiction. All people, locations, events, and situations are portrayed to the best of the author's memory.

All Scripture quotations, unless otherwise indicated, are taken from the Holy Bible, New International Version®, NIV® Copyright © 1973, 1978, 1984, 2011 by Biblica, Inc.™ Used by permission. All rights reserved worldwide. www.zondervan.com. The "NIV" and "New International Version" are trademarks registered in the United States Patent and Trademark Office by Biblica, Inc.™

Liberatio Protocol Post Hill PRESS

Post Hill Press
New York • Nashville
posthillpress.com

Published in the United States of America
1 2 3 4 5 6 7 8 9 10

For my daughter, Baby Blake.
Your smile melts my heart.
Dream big, find your purpose, and then move
mountains.
You were made "for such a time as this."

CONTENTS

CHAPTER 1

THE BURNING CHURCH

*"We must learn to live together as brothers
or we will perish together as fools."*

—Rev. Dr. Martin Luther King, Jr.

Beams of sunlight poured through the shutters of my bedroom window. My eyes were closed, but I was already awake as I waited for my official wake-up call—the beautiful little cry of my six-month-old daughter. As young parents, Sean and I had learned that there was no more sleeping in. Baby Blake always made sure Ma-Ma and Da-Da were both up at the crack of dawn!

But I didn't mind it. I knew my time at home in Florida was dwindling, and I would soon have to head back to our nation's capital. This was one of my first weekends home since taking the job of White House press secretary, and I tried to cherish every moment.

When I first took the job, I had gone a full three weeks without seeing Blake. I missed her very first Easter. She missed my 32nd birthday. So that morning, I relished the idea of walking under the small crystal chandelier I had purchased for her and scooping her up from her crib, positioned just beneath a glimmering gold sign that read "Let her sleep. For when she wakes, she will move mountains."

On that Sunday morning, before Blake's cry could summon her parents, I glanced at the illuminated baby monitor and then down at my phone. I saw a voicemail and a text message from a Tampa Police Department detective. "Sorry to bother you. Can you call me when you get a moment? I have important information to give you," the text read. I immediately called the detective, a bit alarmed at the early morning messages.

"Kayleigh, are you at your house in Tampa?" he asked me.

"Yes, I am," I replied.

"We received a tip last night, and we have reason to believe someone is targeting your home, calling for protesters to burn it down. Stay where you are. Don't leave the house. I am coming your way," he said.

My stomach sank. In the past, my family had received hate mail and intimidating phone calls. I knew this had to be taken seriously. My immediate concern was for my daughter and my husband. I was about to head to the Orlando airport in just a few hours. How in the world could I leave my family behind knowing that we were now a target?

In spite of my fear, fortunately, my house would not be the building I watched burn on the evening of May 31st. Instead, the world would soon watch a different, historic building, St. John's Church, lit ablaze as flames climbed high into the night sky during yet another evening of violent riots across the nation. Twenty-four hours after St. John's burned, I would be standing at the yellow and white church alongside President Trump as he proudly held a Bible in one of the most iconic photos of his presidency.

A few days before the riots began, a nine-minute, twenty-nine-second video depicting the murder of George Floyd filled America's television screens. I was with President Trump that Wednesday when he first watched the video. We had just landed in Washington, DC, after a disappointing trip to Cape Canaveral, Florida, where we had hoped to watch the launch of SpaceX Dragon Capsule. It would have been the first launch of American astronauts into space in nearly a decade and a much-needed morale boost for a grieving country. Scrubbed due to weather, we landed at Joint Base Andrews (JBA) without the win we had anticipated.

Standing with President Trump in his personal office space on Air Force One, we watched the video of Floyd's killing together. The president shook his head as he took in the brutal images, indignant over the injustice he was watching. That evening, President Trump announced that he had asked the Federal Bureau of Investigation (FBI) and the Department of Justice (DOJ) to expedite their investigation into the "very sad and tragic death in Minnesota of George Floyd."

"My heart goes out to George's family and friends. Justice will be served!" he wrote.[1]

Despite the Floyd family's emphatic calls for peace, violent riots besieged the nation, including in my hometown of Tampa.[2] By Saturday night, the National Guard had been called on to address the rioting in seventeen states and Washington, DC.[3] In Tampa, rioters used crowbars to smash the glass doors of a RaceTrac store, also looting a CVS, an AT&T store, and a jewelry store.[4] They lit a Mobil gas station ablaze and set a Champs Sports on fire as it "burn[t] out of control."[5] My family and I watched on our televisions as part of our city went up in flames.

All of these images played in my mind as I waited for the detective to reach my home that last Sunday morning in May. When the detective arrived, he sat at my glass kitchen table and detailed that someone had posted a picture of the Mobil gas station on fire alongside my home address. "Does your family have a place to go? You need to get out of here," the detective instructed. We did just that. The detective departed, and I began to pack a bag for Blake, tossing her pink plastic bottles and brightly colored clothing into a bag. I felt an urgency to leave.

While I was packing, I received a call from my boss, President Trump. He was rightfully perturbed by a piece in the *New York Times*. The *Times* falsely stated that "[a]s several more cities erupted in street protests on Friday night after the killing of George Floyd.... Mr. Trump made no appeal for calm."[6]

"That is completely inaccurate," I told President Trump. "I will try and get it fixed."

Not only had President Trump called for peace, he spent almost ten minutes of his speech at Kennedy Space Center pleading for unity and calm.[7] TEN minutes! I saw it firsthand on Saturday, when Sean, Blake, and I drove to Cape Canaveral, Florida, where we accompanied the president to watch the launch of SpaceX Dragon Capsule. Unlike Wednesday's scrubbed launch, this one had a fifty-fifty chance of takeoff.[8] This time, however, the weather was on our side. We stared up into the sky in amazement as we witnessed the launch of the first new manned spacecraft in about four decades—a huge American triumph.[9]

But knowing that the nation was also witnessing American carnage in our streets, President Trump made the first portion of his speech a call for peace and justice. He called the death of George Floyd "a grave tragedy" and then said this: "I stand before you as a friend and ally to every American seeking justice and peace and I stand before you in firm opposition to anyone exploiting this tragedy to loot, rob, attack and menace. Healing, not hatred, justice, not chaos, are the mission at hand."[10] Unsurprisingly, none of this made it into the *New York Times* piece. Instead, a blatant falsehood did, alleging President Trump had not made a call for "calm."

I made these points to the president during our phone call that Sunday morning and then continued to prepare my family to leave our home. Sean packed up his guns, and I gathered our valuables. We wanted to make sure that we removed our important items in the event our house was ransacked. As my husband helped to load our bags into his black Ford F-250 truck, I fielded more calls from both the president and the reporter, imploring the writer to change his story to reflect the truth while giving the president regular updates on my progress. I also received a text message from my principal assistant press secretary, Chad Gilmartin: "Let me know if you want Lyndee [my executive assistant] and I to find someone to drive you from the airport home, if you don't want to take an Uber!"

"I think it should be fine. I land late, at like 9:50," I replied.

Chad had noticed the protests, some violent, overwhelming DC as evening approached and suggested I find secure transportation, but I buried my head in the sand, dismissing Chad's message and focusing entirely on making sure my family was secure in Florida. We finally loaded up and left our Tampa home that afternoon. Sean backed out of our driveway, pulling away from our red brick two-story home. We crossed paths with a police car as we left. The officer and patrol car now sat on the street, monitoring our house around the clock.

I sat in the backseat alongside Blake as we began our roughly hour-and-a-half-long drive to the Orlando airport. During the ride, I tried to balance the concern for my family with the demands of my job. Doing everything I could to keep my infant daughter peaceful, I held a pink pacifier to her lips while taking yet another rotation of calls from President Trump and a reporter. The situation had escalated from just a few hours earlier when I tried to correct an inaccurate detail. Now, per an "anonymous source," a reporter claimed to have information that President Trump had been evacuated to an underground bunker amid violent protests Friday night happening just beyond the White House's front gate.

The move to the bunker, formally called the Presidential Emergency Operations Center, would evoke comparisons to September 11th, when then-Vice President Dick Cheney was escorted to the protected location.[11] This was a big story and a massive leak coming out of the White House. The Friday night bunker movement occurred amid a series of chaotic events that transpired that evening. On the evening the president was moved to the bunker, my husband and I went to dinner with our little one at a nearby restaurant in Tampa. We sat down with Blake at a beautiful table in the dimly lit steakhouse. At the moment, my biggest concern was keeping my little one quiet and ordering a hard-earned dish of cheesy au gratin potatoes. That quickly changed when I received a text message from a colleague in White House Operations: "Kayleigh - pls call me when you can. All good, but want to fill you in on a situation at WH."

Soon after, I received a call from Deputy Chief of Staff for Operations Tony Ornato. Protesters had knocked down temporary barricades surrounding the White House. The activity had prompted a brief lockdown of the White House facility, corralling press inside the West Wing along with White House staff. Running to and from my table that evening desperate to find a quiet place, I continued to receive messages from reporters and colleagues, including a call from President Trump. In between calls, I tried my best to grab a bite of bread and salad!

Later that Friday night, protests turned to riots nationwide. Upon returning home from dinner, I turned on my TV and watched violent interactions between rioters and police officers in Minneapolis, Atlanta, New York, and in metro areas across the country.

Businesses were looted; buildings set ablaze; and two people even lost their lives, leading one reporter to ask, "Is the United States coming apart?"[12]

It certainly felt like it.

I thought through the events of the weekend as I rode to the airport on Sunday afternoon. On the way there, I received another message from Chad: "Hey just an fyi - I just tried to Uber downtown and it was incredibly difficult. Roads blocked, shattered glass and spray paint everywhere, protesters in the streets. I could not imagine that the conditions will improve by 10 p.m. tonight - especially since your place is right there."

I reluctantly obliged to arranging a car, more concerned about my family and the impending bunker story than my mode of transportation upon arriving in DC.

Just before takeoff in the Orlando airport, I received yet another message from Chad: "Kayleigh, this is filmed from the front door of your building. There is a mob at your front door." Underneath his message was a tweet from a reporter, featuring a twenty-one-second video filmed from the front door of the apartment building I lived in just one block from the White House.[13] The video depicted agitators fleeing in the streets as cops ran toward some type of exploding projectile. I was stunned by the images. It looked like total and complete mayhem—just steps from the White House.

We decided that I should not stay in DC amid these violent protests. My assistant, Lyndee, contacted White House Operations, which agreed that I should stay out in Old Town Alexandria, Virginia. My decision was reinforced by an earlier public safety alert issued in the area. "Mayor Bowser is ordering a citywide curfew for the District of Columbia from 11:00 p.m. on Sunday, May 31, until 6:00 a.m. on Monday, June 1. She has also activated the DC

National Guard to support the Metropolitan Police Department," the message read.[14]

Now aboard my flight awaiting departure, I began to prepare for the next day's White House press briefing, reviewing the rough draft binder that my staff sent me. I worked through various topics that could come up when President Trump called my phone. Answering with many people in close proximity, I whispered into the phone to the White House operator, "Please, tell President Trump I'm on a flight but will call him when I land." I spent the rest of the flight anxious to return the president's call, but I distracted myself by coming up with potential briefing questions to walk through with my team.

One of the keys to success for a White House press briefing was identifying lines of questioning in advance and anticipating counterarguments. The slogan for my press shop that I articulated to my team on day one was clear: "Offense Only." Playing defense with a press corps that often made their partisan disposition clear was a recipe for disaster. Just as a lawyer would approach a case, our press shop would be on offense, thinking ahead, over-preparing, and having more information rather than less.

Tomorrow's briefing, however, would be different than any other typical day. As the nation appeared more divided than ever, I told my team, "Intro tomorrow will be about coming together. I have a rough outline. I will highlight random acts of kindness that police officers did for protesters and vice versa. I have a few examples. We will end with this quote from MLK: 'We must all learn to live together as brothers or we will all perish together as fools.'"[15]

Upon landing, I rushed to the car waiting to take me to Virginia and returned the president's call. We discussed the bunker story and the media reaction. "How's it playing?" President Trump would often call to ask me after a big news story broke. Arriving at my hotel, I hung up with the president, checked in, and then headed to CVS. I had no suitcase with me since I had flown back to Florida last minute after a trip with the vice president to Atlanta, Georgia. Though I only had a small purse for my overnight trip, I managed to wrangle a toothbrush, a box of Cheez-Its, and a bottle of red wine for my room.

I was preparing to go to sleep around 10:30 p.m. when Fox News' Kevin Corke reported that St. John's Church in Washington, DC, was burning. "*What? This can't be right!*" I thought. Surely enough, the television displayed horrible footage of the historic church, just outside the front gates of the White House, in flames. The basement nursery had been set on fire, and now deep orange flares and billowing smoke filled the air.

Was this the United States of America?

I questioned whether we should do the briefing the next day or instead let the president take the lead on messaging during this perilous time, but Chad, one of my closest aides on the press team, urged me to keep the briefing. I continued to watch the violent images before receiving another call from President Trump. He instructed me to keep the briefing and expressed confidence in my ability to articulate the administration's response to the events that were unfolding.

While I watched St. John's Church burn, I began to research the history of this church—a church just outside the White House that I passed almost daily. Built in 1815, St. John's Church had become known as "the Church of the Presidents" since every commander in chief going back to James Madison had attended the charming yellow church in Lafayette Square.[16] Sitting atop this National Historic Landmark is a one-thousand-pound bell crafted by Paul Revere's son.[17] So much history had happened in this building, now ablaze with fire reaching high into the dark night sky.

One piece of history in particular stuck out to me as I read about the church. In 1963, St. John's rector, Reverend John C. Harper, was told that he needed to close the church ahead of the famous March on Washington since "it might be a bloodbath."[18] Rather than closing, Harper insisted on keeping the church open. And as nearly a quarter of a million men and women marched on Washington asking for equal rights, these were the words being sung from St. John's:

"One family on Earth are we
Throughout its widest span:
O help us everywhere to see the brotherhood of man."[19]

Standing in support of the marchers and Rev. Dr. Martin Luther King Jr. as he gave his famous "I Have a Dream" speech, Harper declared, "This church building is open, as it has always been, to all who want to worship here. The ministry of this parish is extended to any who seek it. Our fellowship with one another has no limitations whatsoever."[20]

The irony was not lost upon me. St. John's Church had supported the peaceful march for equality. Now, rioters—purportedly advocating for justice—were burning a historic building that had supported Dr. King and the civil rights movement. I knew immediately that this analogy had to be a part of my briefing the next day.

I expressed to my team how important tomorrow's briefing would be.

"We have a real chance to heal the nation," I told Chad before heading to sleep.

⌒◢⌒

I WOKE UP ON the morning of June 1st in my Virginia hotel room, rushing to make it back to my DC apartment in time to grab a dress for work and pack a bag in the event that I had to stay outside the city for a second night. As we neared my apartment, adjacent to the White House, I was stunned. "ACAB," standing for "All Cops Are Bastards," was spray-painted all across federal government buildings alongside the images of pigs. I could not believe what I was seeing. Washington, DC, looked like a war zone.

I went into my apartment building, quickly packed a bag, and left for the White House with a sense of conviction and purpose, having seen the violent graffiti sprayed across the city. My conviction was enforced even more when I passed the Department of Veterans Affairs on my way in to the White House. Windows were broken. "ACAB" was spray-painted prominently over a Department of Veteran Affairs sign. How did this make sense? Upset over injustice, the protesters had decided to deface our nation's veterans?

First, a church.

Now, our veterans.

Though all of this stirred a sense of indignation inside me, I knew that it was imperative that I hit the right tone in the afternoon briefing. I prayed. I reflected on the moment. I had one goal: bring the nation together.

When I arrived at the White House, President Trump was understandably upset that a historic church in America's seat of government had burned on his watch. The media liked to portray President Trump as angry and menacing, but during my time, I found him to be just the opposite. He was a hard worker, generally amicable, and typically good at lightening the mood. In the aftermath of St. John's Church burning amid violent riots, President Trump's usual light mood was much heavier. I watched as he sent one unilateral message to those in charge of federal law enforcement: secure our streets.

I left our meeting with a distinct sense of how to use my time at the podium. I would continue to acknowledge the injustice we all watched in that nine-minute, twenty-nine-second video of George Floyd losing his life. I would also call for calm and peace ahead of a night with anticipated protests. As I did before every briefing, I sat with my two top advisors—Chad Gilmartin and Julia Hahn, Deputy White House Communications Director. We ran through animating themes of the briefing and potential questions, scrutinizing every single possible scenario.

During our prep time, Julia made a salient point: we did not have a communications problem, but a policy one. Americans wanted law and order, not churches burning. "What is the deliverable? What authorities are we using to solve the problem? What can be done from a law enforcement perspective?" she asked me.

In the briefing, I endeavored to provide answers.

"Good afternoon, everyone. The president has made clear that what we are seeing on America's streets is unacceptable. Violence, looting, anarchy, lawlessness are not to be tolerated, plain and simple. These criminal acts are not protest. They are not statements. These are crimes that harm innocent Americans," I began.[21]

I went on to emphasize a solution-oriented approach. "President Trump is demanding action to protect American citizens, to protect American businesses. Seventeen thousand National Guard are deployed in twenty-four states, but according to General Milley, only two states have deployed more than a thousand. There are 350,000 National Guard available overall, and for the lawlessness we are seeing, far more needs to be done." In other words, states needed to step up and request the National Guard presence available to them.

"With that, I'll take questions."

The first question was a predictable one. "Where is the president? Why has he not delivered an address to the nation, as many of his predecessors have in a time of domestic crisis?"

It was an interesting question and one that we had pondered in the White House. I recall Senior Advisor Jared Kushner's input on the issue. "A national address won't stop anarchists," he said. He was exactly right. President Trump was focused on actions, not words. Besides, no matter what the president said from the Oval Office, the media coverage would not change. Case in point: he had made a nearly ten-minute call for peace at Kennedy Space Center, and the *New York Times* just ignored it. In the interest of the People, President Trump needed to act, not talk.

Taking Jared's point to the podium, I answered, "The president, as recently as forty-eight hours ago, was out talking about what a tragedy the death of George Floyd was, how it has weighed on his heart, and how he encourages peace and lawfulness in our streets and peaceful protest.... Continual statements—as he's made day and day and day again—they don't stop anarchy. What stops anarchy is action, and that's what the president is working on right now."

The questions that came were the typical "gotcha" questions.

"He was literally put in a bunker on Friday night by the Secret Service. I mean, would you agree that he is hiding out on this issue?" one reporter asked.

What? The premise of the question was ridiculous!

"I would not agree with that at all," I said. "Look, I was on the phone with the president at least half a dozen times yesterday, and every time I talked to him, he was telling me about a different action he had taken, whether it was talking to a governor about this or a foreign leader about ventilators."

In that June 1st briefing, finally, I was asked the question I had been hoping for: "A particularly egregious act—St. John's Church, 'Church of the Presidents,' was targeted last night. Graffiti all over it. Set on fire. What is the president's reaction to that, please?"

"It's hurtful, honestly," I answered. "I think it's hurtful on a number of levels. Look, the VA was defaced. Literally, the word 'veteran' spray-painted out of the placard in front of the Department of Veteran Affairs. The Lincoln Memorial defaced. How does that make much sense? The place where the March on Washington began. That moment—that momentous occasion in the history of civil rights—that memorial was defaced last night. That doesn't honor the legacy of George Floyd. It doesn't. And certainly not the burning of St. John's Church."

✐

MY CALLS FOR PEACE were indeed merited. Tragically, the violent protests continued each night, and on Tuesday, June 2, 2020—just a day after my Monday briefing—a seventy-seven-year-old retired police captain was murdered in St. Louis, Missouri. At about 2:30 a.m., David Dorn went to check on his friend's pawn shop, Lee's Pawn & Jewelry, when looters shot him to death. His murder was broadcast on Facebook Live. The footage was horrifying. Dorn was on his back, cell phone still in his hand, as the last few moments of his life are graphically recorded.[22]

After seeing this footage online, Chad called me. "The president needs to see this," he said. I hung up with Chad to make a call to the president.

"Hi, this is Kayleigh, calling for President Trump," I told the switchboard operator, as I sat on the beige leather couch of my DC apartment.

"One second," she replied.

After a few moments of holding, she said, "Kayleigh, the president."

"Hi Kayleigh," President Trump said. "What's going on?"

I told him about the sad footage depicting the last few moments of Officer Dorn's life.

"Tell Dan to put out a tweet honoring his life," President Trump instructed.

Shortly after our conversation came the tweet: "Our highest respect to the family of David Dorn, a Great Police Captain from St. Louis, who was viciously shot and killed by despicable looters last night. We honor our police officers, perhaps more than ever before. Thank you!"

The next day, I decided that we would use the White House podium to acknowledge the life of David Dorn. We would also, again, condemn the killing of George Floyd. We hoped to make the point that injustice is injustice, and it should be recognized wherever it is found, including amid violent riots.

Standing at the podium the next day, I said, "In the famous 'I Have a Dream' speech by Reverend Dr. Martin Luther King, he said this: 'We must not allow our creative protest to degenerate into physical violence. Again and again, we must rise to the majestic heights of meeting physical force with soul force.'…Important words, important actions from an American hero who contributed to make this nation the greatest on earth."[23]

I then transitioned to the recent events that transpired. "With that in mind, we must remember to recognize the lives lost, the passing of George Floyd who was killed unjustly—in a horrific video that we have all seen. And we must also remember the passing of police captain David Dorn yesterday, who was shot and killed by looters in St. Louis, in an absolute tragedy."

As I spoke, "in memory of" graphics were displayed on the screens just behind me.

"George Floyd, 1973-2020," one said.

"David Dorn, 1943-2020," said the other.

I concluded my introduction by saying, "Dorn was a hero and an unfortunate casualty in the riots we have seen. Our hearts are with his family."

Unsurprisingly, I did not receive one question about the passing of David Dorn or the myriad other police targeted and injured amid protests—four police officers shot in St. Louis, an officer in Las Vegas shot in the head and on life support, a cop beat up by a crowd in New York, and countless others injured across the country. I proactively brought out these facts, but violence against officers was never the focus of the White House press corps, and therein lay the problem. If we all endeavored to recognize loss wherever it occurs, rather than taking sides, we would be far better off.

To that end, one of the most emotional days I had in the White House was June 16, 2020. It was at a time when our nation felt so broken—ravaged by a pandemic, incurring months of lockdowns, and now a summer of violent protest. As a country, we felt overwhelmed. As an individual, I felt beleaguered.

Amid the chaos, President Trump was prepared to sign an executive order on policing that Tuesday morning. Rather than acceding to the calls of the left to "defund the police," the order aimed to direct federal funds to police departments that met the highest standards and that engaged in de-escalation training. It incentivized departments to ban choke holds "except if an officer's life is at risk," and it created an information sharing mechanism so that credible abuses by officers would be known to departments during the hiring process.[24]

It was a commonsense executive order.

President Trump would sign the order in the Rose Garden, flanked by law enforcement professionals in a show of support. But prior to the signing, President Trump was set to meet with families who lost their loved ones in a deadly interaction with a police officer. I planned to attend the meeting.

Knowing this meeting was about to start, I hastily left the West Wing and traversed the West Wing Colonnade, heading in the direction of the Residence. I entered the State Dining Room, hoping I was not too late. The State Dining Room was an elaborate but stately room located below the Executive Residence. Often used for formal dinners in the White House, the State Dining Room had welcomed French president Emmanuel Macron for the first state dinner of President Trump's term. Thirteen candlelit tables dotted the room with gold-plated settings and warm lighting, illuminating the two fireplaces on either side of the room. That first state dinner was roughly two years earlier, long before my tenure as press secretary began.

Our country was in a far different place. Businesses had shuttered their doors as COVID-19 ravaged the nation. Violent protests were a nightly occurrence. Our nation was enduring so much pain, as this meeting would make clear. When I entered the State Dining Room, you could not just feel the emotion, you could hear it. Arriving just after the meeting had commenced, families had begun to share the story of how they lost their loved one.

President Trump was seated in the center of the room surrounded by eight families. I quietly took a seat near the back. As loved ones recounted their stories of loss, you could see their tears, hear their cries. An older lady near me was sobbing, going through an entire box of tissues. One father detailed that his deceased son was a military veteran who had proudly served in the United States Army. A grandmother to another victim said, "One day, I'll have to explain to my grandchild how her father died."

Her remark reminded me of remarks that Rob Weinbrenner had made when he talked about the killing of his son, Justin, an off-duty police officer who courageously confronted a gunman and lost his life because of it. Justin left behind a beautiful young daughter named Charlee. In his victim impact statement, Rob said this to the courtroom: "Now [Charlee] will have to learn to do things without her Dad. She couldn't invite him to her preschool this year the day they had donuts with Dad. All the other kids were there with their dad. I went in his place… She had to start her first day of Kindergarten without her dad. I went in his place."[25] Both Rob, a grandfather, and the grandmother who I listened to in the State Dining Room had something in common: earth-shattering loss.

As the tearful meeting was concluding, I noticed one mother across the room. She was sitting and blankly staring into the distance, her pain so evident. With the meeting now over, attendees got up and spoke to one another, but I noticed this mother still sitting in her chair. Something inside compelled me to go up to her.

Making my way across the room, I was stopped by an elected official who wanted to introduce herself. We spoke briefly, but I broke away—intent on speaking to this mother, still sitting stationary.

"Ma'am I'm praying for you," I said to the woman, slightly crouching down to just above eye level.

She looked at me and started to cry.

I cried too.

"May I hug you?" I asked.

She nodded, and I bent further down to hug her.

"Jesus Christ can overcome all things. I'm praying for you," I shared before I walked away.

I walked back to the West Wing, emotional from the exchange that I had just had.

As I exited the central area of the White House and walked along the outdoor colonnade, I noticed the Rose Garden was already set for the upcoming press conference, where President Trump would sign the policing executive order. The press was there. I turned my head to the right and toward the wall, not wanting them to see my tears.

I got back to my office and sat at my desk, taking a second to breathe and dry my eyes. I opened my *Jesus Calling* devotional to find the most appropriate message for that day: "Resolution."

It was perfectly relevant. On this earth, there would be grave injustice—be it an officer who is killed in the line of duty or George Floyd taking his final breath with a knee on his neck. Injustice would always be with us. No protest or executive order or piece of legislation could change that. Through Christ is where we find "resolution" to the injustices we face that can never be fully rectified in the here and now. And it is in viewing one another through the eyes of Christ that we can heal our divisions.

CHAPTER 2

THE PATH TO THE PODIUM

"As iron sharpens iron, so one person sharpens another."

—Proverbs 27:17

Growing up, my dad always used the term "worldview." He said that everyone had one whether they knew it or not. I didn't quite understand that concept fully until I went out on my own. As I went to Washington, DC, to New York City, and then eventually to Oxford University, where I spent my junior year of college, the term crystalized. I was a Christian. I was a conservative. This was my worldview. It was at the central core of my being, firmly sewn within me. It is the prism through which I see the world. As I left my home, I encountered contrasting worldviews. It would be up to me how to handle these moments. My first "tutorial" at Oxford University was just such an encounter.

Unlike in American universities, where lectures were the main source of learning, at Oxford University, one-on-one time with professors—known there as "tutors"—served as the focus. Each week, you were expected to write either one or two ten-page papers.

But rather than your professor scribbling down a grade and a few notes, you were instead instructed to read your work out loud in a "tutorial" setting with, at most, one other student. Your tutor, a highly credentialed and well-studied academic, would stop you along the way, challenge your ideas, and ask you to explain your perspective or provide your sourcing. If you thought my press briefings were intense, think again! The tutorial far eclipsed the press briefing in terms of difficulty. Preparing for these tense encounters certainly shaped the way I prepared before I went to the podium.

My first tutorial was brutal, and I still remember it vividly. That day, I ascended the circuitous brown staircase with an appropriate level of angst, unaware of the challenge that waited at the perch of the tower I was climbing. Known as the "City of Dreaming Spires" for its soaring, castle-like structures, Oxford, England, was a magical little town, rich in history but rigorous in academics. As a student at Georgetown University School of Foreign Service, I had intentionally sought out a year at Oxford University for a reason: I wanted to fine-tune a very specific skill—the art of debating. As a staunch conservative and Christian, I did not look to change my views, but I certainly wanted them countered. I wanted to learn to defend my deeply held convictions intelligently, and that could only happen if I was challenged. And challenged I was.

As I traversed the old staircase of the twelfth-century library that fall day, I finally arrived at my first tutorial, expecting a challenging setting but blissfully unaware of the back and forth about to come. I sat across the desk from my tutor, alongside one other student, and soon began to read my paper out loud. As I read my first international relations paper, I was uncertain whether my voice was truly shaking or if it was all in my head. Several times throughout my oration, my tutor stopped me and scrupulously challenged my thoughts. It was a rigorous exchange, and I left that tutorial in tears, calling my mom to describe the thought-provoking conversation. I was determined to come back stronger.

It became clear over the course of our sessions that my tutor had a very different outlook than my own. As a former representative of the Palestinian Liberation Organization, she challenged many of my ideas, not just that day but in our sessions that followed. Ultimately, she made me better. I look back on our tutorials fondly because she taught me to listen to alternative perspectives. To this day, I still hold the same worldview—a Christian, a conservative, a staunch supporter of Israel—but I am better for having listened and understood. My Oxford tutorials taught me to challenge my ideas, to thoroughly source my work, and—importantly—to anticipate counterarguments, a skill that comes in quite handy in preparing for a White House press briefing.

❦

MY WORLDVIEW WAS SHAPED by two loving parents who selflessly invested themselves in each of their children, creating a faith-based and family-centered environment for their three kids. I was born in Jacksonville, Florida; however, my parents moved to Plant City, Florida, a twenty-thousand-person town along Interstate 4, shortly after I was born. Plant City, affectionately known as the "Winter Strawberry Capital of the World," is a small town in central Florida with warm, salt-of-the-earth people. Every year in late February or early March, the town congregates to celebrate its cherished agricultural product at the Florida Strawberry Festival. Strawberry shortcake, of course, is plentiful, as is country music. From Garth Brooks and Toby Keith to Big & Rich and Rascal Flatts, country's hottest celebrities descended—for a moment in time—upon my home in Plant City, Florida.

In my early years, I attended Walden Lake Elementary School, the local public school where my mom was a teacher. Like many young children, my memories of the time are sparse, but a few stand out. I recall chanting for Bob Dole on the playground in 1996 as an eight-year-old girl. Ahead of the November election, my elementary school held a mock election. Much to my chagrin, Bill Clinton won our school's vote tally, beating Dole in a landslide. When I found out my brother, Michael, voted for Clinton because he liked the sound of his name, I refused to speak to my younger brother for days. In the aftermath of the election, I took it upon myself to run down the hill behind my house and onto the golf course, where I glued signs to the water cooler articulating my disapproval of the Clinton White House.

Weekdays in my small town centered around the little league field. In the fall, my brother and his teammates would burst through a paper sign spanned across the goalpost, ready to take the field for the Plant City Dolphins. Clad in my teal and orange, I was proud to be a cheerleader shouting from the sidelines. In the spring, my brother played baseball, and I tried one bout at softball. One problem, though: instead of hitting the ball, the ball hit me. I stuck out the season, but after one year, I proudly transitioned from the mound to the concession stand, where I was pleased to be making five dollars an hour.

On weeknights, it was a good night if I got to ditch doing the dishes at the sink overlooking my family's dining room table and instead feast at Hungry Howie's or the Chinese buffet. Whether at home or at a restaurant, family dinners were a nightly occurrence, and they always began with prayer. "Dear Jesus, we thank YOU for this day. We thank you for this meal. We love you Lord. Protect this family." These values stayed with me all through my life, no matter where I was—Plant City or Washington, DC, Tampa or New York City.

My upbringing in Plant City was wholesome and family-oriented, but it was not free of trial. I learned about loss early on when a sweet angel in our community, Megan Carpenter, got cancer at eleven years old. Between surgeries and chemotherapy, Megan always engaged with the community. After our Dolphin football games, we would attend "Dolphin Dances," where the town would dance to the Macarena. Megan would attend, battling a horrid disease far too young. When we would meet at a neighbor's home for four-wheeling and traditional Southern cooking—warm, buttered biscuits and collard greens—Megan would be there too. She had a smile on her face, no matter the circumstance—losing her hair or feeling weak. After six years of battling cancer, Megan went to be with Jesus. "Don't be mad at God. He's watching after us," she told her family. Megan might have passed, but her faith lives on in this community and beyond.

At fifth grade, I left public school for a private Catholic school in Tampa called the Academy of the Holy Names. In addition to my Catholic schooling, every Sunday, my family attended our Southern Baptist church, and on Wednesdays, I went to youth group. The pews of my local church and the Biblical truths shared from its pulpit provided my spiritual grounding and kept me centered through high school, college, and my adult life.

While my church instilled in me a love for Christ, I also developed a political foundation from a very young age. This political foundation grew during my rides in my dad's truck, where we would listen to *The Rush Limbaugh Show*. Rush's passion, conviction, and unwavering confidence lit a fire within me—a spark that would reverberate through my entire future professional life. When I carpooled with fellow classmates either to my all-girls Catholic high

25

school or to cheerleading practice at the all boy's companion school, my passengers knew that Rush Limbaugh would be the soundtrack in my little black car.

On Friday nights during high school, you could find me on the track with pom-poms cheering on the Jesuit Tigers football team, but on Saturdays, I dropped the pom-poms for a rolling backpack as I headed in to debate tournaments. Equipped with a Ronald Reagan book of quotes, I began every opening debate salvo with a word of wisdom from the Gipper. My love of politics ultimately manifested itself in state debate championships and a trip to nationals in Philadelphia, where I did not win, but I had found a passion.

While a senior in high school, I knew there was only one college for me: Georgetown University. Georgetown, known for its academic excellence, was set right in the heart of our nation's capital. It offered the perfect opportunity to grow intellectually while also having access to the halls of Congress and the White House—both branches of government I would eventually intern at as a student at Georgetown. In high school, I had interned for the Bush-Cheney 2004 presidential campaign and Tom Gallagher's gubernatorial campaign. These experiences set the stage for me to intern in the halls of Congress for Congressman Adam Putnam, where I regularly gave tours to constituents from my home state.

Following my congressional internship, I considered applying to intern in the Senate but ultimately set my sights on the White House. It was the final year of President George W. Bush's administration, and, for a college student, a White House internship offered an up-close experience in the world's most powerful building. At this point, I had completed several internships in Republican politics, which paved the way for me to receive an internship in the White House Office of Media Affairs. While most White House interns took a semester off to devote to the internship, I wanted to keep on track with my studies and opted to be a full-time intern and full-time student. Forgoing spring break and other typical college activities, my work began before the sun would rise, and my studies ended long after sunset. Departing for the White House early in the morning while it was still dark, I would call my mom and nervously walk to the big wrought iron gate at the front of Georgetown to wait for a taxi. Upon arrival at the White House, I would walk to the Secret Service checkpoint and tell my mom, "Hold on one second. I need to put you through security." Sending the phone through the security belt with my other belongings, I would gather my items and scurry off to my desk to start work.

During my time as a White House intern, opportunities abounded—like the time when I saw a White House press briefing live. I will never forget it. Dana Perino was the White House press secretary as I stood in the back of the room and watched her field the reporters' questions. I was completely mesmerized and enthralled by the moment. At that point, I would have never envisioned that just over a decade later, I would be the one taking questions from behind that very podium.

For all the good times in the White House, though, there were also tough ones. As a wide-eyed go-getter, I strived for perfection. Perfection, as we all know, is unattainable, and there were times I was far from perfect. One time, I had been given a relatively simple task—faxing the president's schedule to a group of local reporters on the ground. I sent the fax, checking the item off my list, but perhaps prematurely. The next day, my boss informed me that half of the press on the president's trip to Louisiana didn't have his schedule because I had failed to send it. On that stressful day, I hurried across the checkered floors of the Old Executive Office Building, the building in the White House complex just across from the West Wing, and locked myself in a bathroom stall where I cried to my mom. But I picked up my head and moved on, determined to do better.

My determination drove my success. After completing my White House internship and having that incredible encounter in the briefing room, I explored the media landscape. Observing the Fox News White House correspondent during the press briefing I had attended piqued my interest, and an internship at Fox News in New York City seemed like an exhilarating new adventure. I applied to Fox and landed a spot with the coveted prime-time show *Hannity & Colmes*.

As I knew all too well at this point, landing the internship was only half the battle; thriving in it was most important. In almost any internship, your bosses are busy, and it's your job to make yourself useful to the operation. At Fox, I had been given small tasks like filing tapes and arranging guests, but I felt strongly that I could be even more helpful. I wanted to take a crack at writing the short opening script to the show. Rather than asking for the opportunity, I just did it. Each morning, I attempted to write the opening script and left a copy on the producer's desk. After doing this a few times, he finally said, "Hey, you're pretty good at this. Why don't you keep doing this every day? I'll even let you go down and lead the editing process." He empowered me because I showed him my capability, and in the process, I learned a good life lesson: opportunity won't find you, you must find it.

My opportunity at Fox eventually led to another. The subsequent summer I returned for a second internship, this time with *Huckabee*. This internship turned into a job as a production assistant, and I spent three years learning from Governor Huckabee, a man of great faith, deep intellect, and relatability. He knew how to distill facts in a way that the American public understood. He taught me to take my academic background and make it relatable and digestible to the American public.

Ironically (or perhaps God-ordained), working for Governor Huckabee's show also meant that I would be crossing paths with his incredibly talented and wonderful daughter, Sarah Huckabee Sanders. Just like when I had seen Dana Perino taking questions from the podium—not knowing I would one day be there—I was now in close proximity to Sarah Sanders, not knowing that she would be taking the podium before me and setting a great example in doing so.

Through my internships in New York City and Washington, DC, and while at Georgetown and Oxford, I encountered a variety of different perspectives. In these settings, students and peers had passionately held viewpoints, oftentimes differing from my own. This environment made me better. Every challenging conversation, every professor with a viewpoint contrary to mine, only served as a training ground for the day I would take to the White House podium and encounter a level of hostility rarely seen in academia but far too common on the sets of CNN. Unfortunately, I fear that, for today's college students, for our future generation of leaders, political figures, and press secretaries, the challenging and healthy sparring grounds of universities I found is becoming a thing of the past. That would become abundantly clear during my time at Harvard Law School.

✤

AFTER THREE YEARS OF working at Fox and learning how to communicate effectively through the televised medium, I decided it was time to pursue law school, where I could further enhance my debating and research skills. Eager to return to my home state and the city where my dad grew up, I chose to attend the University of Miami School of

Law. Miami law school had offered me a scholarship, and the Coral Gables campus had the added benefit of being near my Mema—my sweet grandmother whom I adored. Intent on getting the most I could out of law school, I spent nearly every waking minute either in class or reading through various legal cases. The only real time I took for myself was Saturday nights at Mema's house. She would order Miami's famous squared pizza from Frankie's or make a homemade dinner, and we would laugh together over red wine. I would sleep over, head to church the next day, pick up Boston Market for lunch, and get back to work.

My first year in law school was a year of obsessive studying, and it paid off. In fact, when my mom visited my apartment, she joked that she was a little concerned at the hurricane of neon sticky notes that littered my walls. I ended my first year of law school number one in my class. This had nothing to do with natural ability, but it had everything to do with hard work. As my dad always said, quoting Tim Notke, a high school basketball coach, "Hard work beats talent when talent doesn't work hard."[1] That first year of law school, I worked hard.

My time in Florida, unfortunately, was short-lived. Recognizing my potential, a professor at my law school urged me to transfer. "We have a great school here," he noted. "But with grades like these, you could go anywhere. You deserve those opportunities, even if it means leaving home." It was wise advice, though hard to hear.

I applied to transfer law schools and was accepted to every top school where I applied, though I did not wait to hear back from Yale since there was only one school I wanted: Harvard Law School (HLS). I had visited HLS while in middle school with a friend. At the top of the steps of the Harvard Law School library, I took a picture in a light blue Harvard sweatshirt with beige capri pants. Standing between towering columns and beneath the Greek etched lettering translated as "Not under man but God and Law," I vowed I would be back.

As the summer of 2014 progressed, I heard back from several schools—Columbia, NYU, UPenn, and Georgetown—but I waited with great anticipation to hear from Harvard. I knew that, in the case of Harvard, I would not get a letter of admittance or denial; rather, I would get a phone call. When I saw a voicemail from Cambridge, Massachusetts, upon landing on a flight, my heart began to flutter. Could this be Harvard?! I called the number back, and much to my disbelief I had been admitted to Harvard Law School. I burst into tears at baggage claim. Even though life took me in a different direction for a while, my intuition that life might take me to Harvard Law eventually came true. God had put that desire in my heart for a reason.

At this point, I had done a fair amount of television, appearing on some Fox shows and also a CNN pilot. The show I primarily appeared on was *Varney & Co.* on Fox Business with Stuart Varney. Stuart, a kind and likeable man with a great sense of humor, had watched me evolve on his set from first year law student at Miami to Harvard transfer. It was a big honor when Stuart announced live on *Varney & Co.* that I had achieved my lifelong dream of being admitted to Harvard Law School. "I know your mom is watching me share this news with our viewers!" Stuart said, a point we still joke about to this day.

At the same time God opened the door to Harvard Law School, He also shut another—for a reason. After being admitted to Harvard, I received an opportunity to appear on ABC's *The View*. The midday show was looking for a new, Republican co-host, and this would be an opportunity to throw my hat in the ring. On August 4, 2014, I appeared on *The View* along with Whoopi Goldberg, Jenny McCarthy, and Nicolle Wallace. As you can imagine, Whoopi and I did not see eye-to-eye and had our fair share of spicy exchanges. Following my appearance, I was invited back to do what they call a "chemistry test"—an off-air filming where the network subs in different potential candidates before selecting one for the spot. When I arrived on set, I met Rosie O'Donnell for the first time—another person who does not necessarily share my views. That may be the understatement of the year! Even so, Rosie was very kind to me, asking questions about my personal life. I told her that I had just been admitted to Harvard Law School, and I recall her saying something along the lines of, "You need to go to Harvard!" In the end, I did not get the spot on *The View*. It wasn't God's plan. God had something bigger for me on the horizon—I would become White House press secretary, though I could not see it then. As the famous Garth Brooks song, "Unanswered Prayers," illustrates, sometimes—later in life—you are thankful for the prayers God chooses not to answer. So I packed my bags, and I headed to Harvard.

Harvard Law School was everything good that I imagined it would be. Tucked away in Cambridge, Massachusetts—known as "the People's Republic of Cambridge" for the town's liberal bent—Harvard was tough, enriching, and humbling. I cherished those crisp, fall mornings. Walking to class along a small pathway, the leaves on the lush trees would change to beautiful tones of red and yellow. Similar to my Oxford tutorials, most law schools, including Harvard, utilized the Socratic method. This entailed a professor calling on a student and grilling that student on the facts of a case or the legal reasoning. You had to be on your toes, as you could be singled out at any moment. It was challenging, but it was also fun.

During my second year on campus, unfortunately, the tempo began to change. In November of 2014, a grand jury in Ferguson, Missouri, announced that it would not charge Officer Darren Wilson in the shooting death of Michael Brown. Following the shooting, cries of "hands up, don't shoot" erupted across the nation. The narrative set in that Wilson shot Brown as he attempted to surrender, hands in the air. This, however, was wholly inaccurate, as President Obama's own Justice Department concluded months after the grand jury decision. In fact, Brown had charged at Wilson, not attempted surrender. "Based on this investigation, the Department has concluded that Darren Wilson's actions do not constitute prosecutable violations," read the Obama-era report.[2]

These facts, however, did little to calm the riots that ravaged the nation or lower the temperature on my Ivy League law school campus. In short, a firestorm erupted. At Harvard, protesters anonymously attacked students, including myself, calling my pro-police viewpoint "vitriolic." They attempted to stifle free discourse by removing signs around school that they disagreed with and targeted faculty for public shaming. They slammed fellow students on an anonymous blog. They even put a physical piece of tape on the wall, demanding that "privileged" speech be placed on one side, and "silenced" speech on another. The words "Freedom of Speech is not neutral" were plastered above the dividing tape.[3] These protesters had one goal: silence opposition.

I catalogued the happenings on Harvard's campus in great detail in my previous book, and I share them briefly here as I believe these tactics are still at work today on many of our college campuses— silencing alternative viewpoints and shaming conservatives willing to speak.[4] To be clear, at Harvard, it wasn't faculty targeting students but students silencing other students, a regrettable and counterproductive reality. Healthy debate had been replaced with outright demonization.

In her confirmation hearings, then-judge, soon-to-be-Justice Amy Coney Barrett described it this way: "When I write an opinion resolving a case, I read every word from the perspective of the losing party. I ask myself how would I view the decision if one of my children was the party I was ruling against: Even though I would not like the result, would I understand that the decision was fairly reasoned and grounded in the law? That is the standard I set for myself in every case, and it is the standard I will follow as long as I am a judge on any court."[5]

Though I am not a judge, I am someone deeply involved in politics, and this appreciation for opposing views does not mean sacrificing my principles or changing my worldview, but it does mean listening to the other side. Indeed, I believe society would be far better off if we did a little more of that. For me, those Oxford tutorials embedded that principle within me and equipped me with the practice of truly listening and engaging alternative perspectives. It's a practice I would carry with me to Harvard Law School, the television sets of CNN, the White House podium, and beyond.

Biblically and spiritually, this concept is summed up this way: "As iron sharpens iron, so one person sharpens another." – Proverbs 27:17. Writer Mel Walker says this verse describes "both friendship and accountability...In Old Testament times, one iron blade was used to sharpen another blade until both became more effective tools. This visual aid of a common implement of work or war provides a practical model for many human relationships."[6] As someone who has spent nearly a decade discussing politics as a television commentator and then as a government official engaging with reporters, "iron sharpening iron" has characterized many of my human relationships. I can say with great certainty that opposing viewpoints have made me better, not just professionally but also personally.

Throughout my career, I've crossed paths with many people with different views—be it Democrat commentator Alan Colmes while I was just an intern at Fox News or Van Jones while I was working at CNN. In the case of both Alan and Van, they became so much more than Democrats whom I would spar with either in a greenroom or on set, they became friends. To me, our interactions represent a type of mutual understanding that would truly behoove society at large if we chose to embrace one another in a similar manner.

"I love your cross!" were the first cheerful words Van Jones said to me as I rounded the corner at CNN and nervously entered the greenroom filled with Democrat commentators. On set, he warmly coached me through primary night television coverage, lending me a mirror so that I could remove the lipstick from my teeth before airtime. Van went on to partner with President Trump in passing landmark criminal justice reform when many other Democrats would not.

"You don't fight fire with fire, you fight it with water," is one of the last things Alan Colmes messaged to me before he tragically passed away at age sixty-six. The veteran television commentator had seen me debating on a fiery CNN panel and thought to send me a wise tip and an encouraging note. Ever since I was a young college student, Alan had supported me. I gathered that he appreciated my willingness to hear the other side of the argument while never caving on principle.

Unfortunately, in today's culture, this kind of amicable relationship between opposing views is less common. Today's discourse—whether in academia or politics—has become so toxic as to venture into the realm of lunacy. A great example is the "Domino's" saga that happened a few months after I became White House press secretary.[7]

Yes, Domino's as in the pizza chain.

In November of 2012, I tweeted this: "FUN FACT: @dominos is wayyyy better than any NYC pizza"

Domino's replied: "@kayleighmcenany That's one heck of a compliment! Thanks for the love! #WEAPPRECIATE IT!"

Now, eight years later—yes, EIGHT years—Rick Wilson, a leftist and a co-founder of the anti-Trump Lincoln Project, decided to tweet the following to Domino's: "You just killed your brand. #ETTD". I found out that "ETTD" stood for "Everything Trump Touches Dies." So here was a liberal, seeking to cancel Domino's for sending a kind tweet to the White House press secretary, nearly a decade before she took the job? Sure. That makes sense.

Domino's began trending on Twitter that evening as users offered their thoughts on the matter with a celebrity chef tweeting, "F--- you @Dominos."[8] I laughed at the crazy replies. "*If only they found my Taco Bell tweets!*" I thought. The Domino's "controversy" got so much attention that evening that someone, presumably, thought to send a Domino's pizza to my home in Florida. I was in DC, but my husband, Sean, told me that someone rang the doorbell of our Florida home at around 11:45 p.m. It was a Domino's pizza man with a pie in his hand. Sean did not answer, so we will never know how that came about!

The next day, Domino's replied to the controversy with this: "Welp. It's unfortunate that thanking a customer for a compliment back in 2012 would be viewed as political. Guess that's 2020 for ya."[9] The next day, I ordered Domino's pizza for the whole press team, and we laughed over the matter in my office.

One thing Domino's got right, and it wasn't a laughing matter per se, was "that's 2020 for ya." Sadly, demonization and derision far too often characterized our interactions rather than the inquisitive but respectful dialogue with opposing views I had come to love. I would experience it firsthand in the White House on far more serious matters than pizza.

CHAPTER 3

THE JOB OFFER

"...for just such a time as this..."
—ESTHER 4:14

If you would have told me that I would be appointed White
House press secretary in April of 2020 during a once-in-a-gener-
ation outbreak of a novel disease just before violent protests beset
the nation, the leader of the free world contracted the virus, and a
Supreme Court Justice passed away weeks before the presidential
election, I would have told you that you were crazy. But that is what
2020 held for my life and for our nation.

In 2016, the first year of President Trump's term, I had decided
to leave media for politics. Departing the CNN sets in New York
City, I relocated to Washington, DC, where I took the job of
national spokesperson for the Republican National Committee.
With midterm elections on the horizon, the RNC offered a great
opportunity for me to fight for Republicans to maintain our major-
ities in the House and Senate. After a high energy 2018 midterm
election cycle, where we unfortunately lost our House majority but
performed well by historical standards, Trump Campaign Manager

Brad Parscale offered me the job of national press secretary for the Trump campaign. I readily accepted the role, eager to travel the country and finally experience those one-of-a-kind Trump rallies.

Throughout 2019 and in the beginning of 2020, it felt like any other presidential election cycle, albeit a bit higher energy with Trump on the ticket. In January of 2020, Lara Trump, Mercedes Schlapp, and I loaded up in a bus and set across snowy Iowa for the first trip in a "Women for Trump" bus tour series. Greeting throngs of excited Iowans, we highlighted President Trump's roaring economy, blissfully unaware of the impending outbreak of COVID-19 on the horizon.

We completed the tour and geared up for the next big event, the annual Conservative Political Action Conference (CPAC), where thousands of conservative activists would aggregate to hear from a variety of leaders in the conservative movement. It was late February, and the coronavirus was mentioned in news reporting but still felt like a distant threat.

"New Chinese virus cases decline, but tracking method revised again," read PBS.[1]

But as time progressed, the headlines grew more concerning. With rapidity, everything began to change. A week after CPAC, while at dinner with my husband in Florida, I learned that someone at CPAC had tested positive for COVID-19. The Trump campaign canceled the upcoming bus tour, and society slowly began to shut down. Little did I know, I would have one more week of working in person in the DC campaign headquarters before everything came to a sudden stop.

That last week in the office, I brought Blake with me to work each day. Dressed in her pink "Future Harvard Freshman" onesie, Blake had a little nursery in the corner of my office that my colleagues and I had assembled for her. A rotating group of friends on the campaign came in and rocked her as I fielded calls from reporters and prepared for television hits. When Blake and I returned to Florida that weekend, we had no idea we were there to stay—at least for a while.

Like swiftly falling dominos, society changed on a dime. The Trump campaign announced that we would all be working remotely. In a span of a few hours one Friday afternoon, all restaurants were suddenly closed in the Sunshine State.[2] That evening when the restaurants closed their doors, my family and I ventured out to the grocery store, forgoing our plans to dine out. The store was almost entirely empty. There was an eerie silence down the once-bustling aisles of the Publix grocery store. America was on the brink of being ravaged by the COVID-19 pandemic, and I was about to have the world's loudest microphone from the podium of the James S. Brady Press Briefing Room.

✇

I STILL REMEMBER WHERE I was when I got that first call, setting off a series of events that would culminate in my moving from the Trump campaign to the Trump White House. It was a sunny day in March. Lockdowns had just been imposed across the nation, and I was riding in the car with my mom and Blake, who was about four months old then. Blake was a regular staple on the campaign trail in her early days. With the great help of my mom, Blake had traveled with me all across the campaign trail to rallies, primaries, and caucuses in Iowa, South Carolina, North Carolina, New Jersey, and beyond.

Now, like the rest of America, we only traveled between home and the grocery store. Our daily treat was a sunny walk through the neighborhood, and our daily appointment viewing was the Coronavirus Task Force briefings, where President Trump, flanked by public health professionals, updated the nation on the state of COVID-19. I watched the briefings with a fine-tooth comb, taking diligent notes along the way. If others watched alongside me, they knew I would press pause on the remote until conversation died down, intent on absorbing every word, every fact the task force was sharing with the nation.

On that March afternoon drive with my mom and Blake, we crossed a bridge overlooking the water, just as my phone began to ring. It was an odd series of numbers that I recognized as the White House switchboard. I had spoken to President Trump a handful of times—in person on the campaign trail and a few times via phone. I was pretty certain this was him calling. I answered, praying that my daughter would stay calm through the call.

It was, indeed, President Trump. This time, though, instead of a complimentary call about a TV hit I had just done or an article I had penned, he asked me a very specific question.

"Would you be interested in being my press secretary?"

Completely stunned, I responded without hesitation. "Yes sir, that would be the honor of my lifetime."

"Mark, get it done," he said. I assumed he was addressing that remark to newly appointed Chief of Staff Mark Meadows.

The phone call was truly unbelievable.

In the weeks that followed that call with the president, there were a series of calls between me, the chief, and others in the White House—including Johnny McEntee, director of the White House Presidential Personnel Office, who was a great advocate for me receiving the position—all culminating in the official phone call that I will never forget. That official offer to become White House press secretary came on a Saturday night. Like so many other Americans during lockdown, my family was engulfed in a newly discovered Netflix series when I saw a call from Mark coming through.

"Hello," I answered, running up the stairs to find a quiet place.

"Kayleigh, I am calling to let you know that we've officially selected you as press secretary," he said.

"I will not let you down, Mark. I promise you that," I assured him.

"I know you won't," he replied.

With a thousand emotions brimming within me, I walked downstairs and shared the news with my family. My mom was the first to find out. She engulfed me in a big hug in our kitchen, the same kitchen that we sat around when I was just out of college and new to the workforce. She would give me advice on how to climb to the next step of my career. Together, we strategized each of my moves, culminating in this moment. I then shared the news with my dad and sister, Ryann, in the living room. Together, we celebrated. My husband, who was driving back from a hunting trip, found out through a phone call. About an hour later, he arrived at my parents' front door and gave me a big hug. It was truly a dream come true, but it was a dream come true happening within a national nightmare.

A few days later, on Tuesday, April 7th, I was announced as the nation's 33rd White House press secretary. My official first day in the role would be less than a week later.

I spent my final few days in Florida fielding calls from soon-to-be White House colleagues. "If you ever get a chance to do a press briefing, leave the room with a winsome smile," one colleague advised. I also spoke to several of my predecessors to seek advice on how to succeed in the role. "Never let the magic of the moment, the honor of walking into the White House leave you," one former press secretary said. "If it ever leaves, it's time to move on." I even read academic journal articles about the best model for setting up a press shop because, yes, I am that much of a nerd!

My challenge, which I was well aware of, was lacking the institutional knowledge of the White House. Yes, I had interned in the Old Executive Office Building—the building across from the West Wing—but I had never worked in the West Wing, like my predecessors Stephanie Grisham and Sarah Sanders. What I did not know, though, I was determined to learn and learn quickly. I knew I had the skill set to succeed, and most importantly, I knew God had put me at this place, in this moment, for a reason.

ON FRIDAY, APRIL 10TH, my husband and I packed up his black Ford F-250 and prepared to head to Washington, DC. I was already renting an apartment in DC near the White House. For the last several years I had lived there, working as RNC national spokesperson before joining the Trump campaign, but I had not been to the nation's capital since the onset of lockdowns. Now that I was under a microscope with the press, given the high profile of my new role, Sean and I determined that it was best to drive the long trek up the northeast corridor. I didn't want to be seen on a crowded flight before even starting the job.

In addition to preparing for my new role those last few days in Florida, I tried to spend as much time as possible with my daughter. As difficult as the decision was, Sean and I agreed that it would be safest to leave Blake in Florida. This meant that when we drove away that Friday, I would have no idea when I would next see my four-month-old. Blake had become my little buddy on the campaign trail, but with the onset of the pandemic, I had no idea when she would be able to travel up to see me.

President Trump, in his first call to me after I became press secretary, made that difficult moment easier. Rather than talking about the demands of my new job, he asked me a question: "Will your daughter be okay? How about your husband?" It meant more than he knew that the leader of the free world would take the time to care about my personal life. He had far bigger things to deal with.

I remember distinctly one of my last days in Florida. I was holding Blake on the couch in front of the television and looking down at her. As I rocked her, I began to cry, knowing that I was just days from leaving her. I watched as my physical tears fell on her tiny body. As the droplets landed on her soft skin, she lit up with a big smile. It was, as I remember, her very first smile. I knew in that moment that it was her way of saying, "Go, Mommy, it will all be okay!" and God's way of giving me reassurance.

As we pulled out of the driveway that Friday morning, my mom assured me that she would bring Blake to DC as soon as she could. I tearfully rode away, knowing that my problems paled in comparison to those of many others, especially those enduring unthinkable loss to COVID-19.

My husband and I began our nearly thirteen-hour drive to Washington. We stopped in Charlotte, North Carolina for the evening to visit family and break up our journey. During our drive, I continued to place calls to former press secretaries to get advice, and of course, I didn't miss a minute of that Friday's Coronavirus Task Force briefing, taking detailed notes on a white legal pad. As we crossed through Georgia, the Carolinas, and Virginia, I thought about the solemn responsibility that lay ahead: communicating with the American People during a global pandemic.

I gazed out the window during our ride and looked at the houses along the road. We drove through tiny little towns in South Georgia, and I thought about how important it was for me to speak to the families in these homes who would be looking to the administration for answers. I wanted to speak directly to them—the everyday, forgotten Americans—not necessarily the DC bubble. For me, it wasn't about schmoozing with reporters and getting caught up in the Washington echo chamber, but instead reaching into the very homes I was looking at, in a way that was understandable, clear, and compassionate.

MONDAY, APRIL 13, 2020, was my first day on the job as White House press secretary. To say that I had great anticipation was an understatement. I had already picked out my outfit—a red blazer with gold buttons, black pants, and red high heels. I was never one to do my nails, usually opting for the short choppy look free of polish. Unable to paint my own nails, I enlisted my husband to give it a go on the eve of my first day. He was a Major League Baseball pitcher after all. He had to have precision and the ability to paint in the lines, right? Wrong! My fingers looked ridiculous, with beige polish dried all along my skin.

"I can't find any nail polish remover, Sean! What do I do?" I proclaimed. We both panicked for a moment before locating a bottle buried deep in a drawer.

That night, I could not sleep as I pondered what my first day would hold. I woke up early that morning and listened to a sermon for motivation. My apartment, located in the Woodward Building, was just steps from the White House. I figured it would be an easy walk to work on my first day, but it was nothing of the sort. I walked through the parking garage and out toward the street to find that it was pouring rain. As it turned out, I would have to travel the perimeter of the White House to go in a specific gate. Briskly walking about three quarters of a mile as barreling sideways rain darted beneath my umbrella was certainly not the first day I envisioned, but here I was!

When I arrived in the West Wing, I was one of the only ones there. My hair was an absolute mess, so I ran to the bathroom and did my best to dry both my hair and the bottom half of my sopping wet pants. I walked into the press secretary's office, an office that I had visited once before but never thought would one day be my own. The large square office had three floor-to-ceiling windows and track lighting along the perimeter of the ceiling. A beautiful gold chandelier with twelve glowing sconces hung in the center of the room. On one side of the office was a coffee table, a couch, and two chairs sitting atop the navy blue carpeted floors. On the other side, just above a round table used for meetings sat several televisions, offering a window into the day's press coverage. Adding to the office's regal beauty was the fact that it was one of the only offices in the West Wing with a fireplace—a fireplace we put to good use during my tenure!

I sat at my desk for the first time, overwhelmed with nerves and in disbelief that this moment had come. Shortly after I arrived in my office, Mark Meadows walked in and set a cake on the round brown table. "My wife, Debbie, wanted your team to have this as a gift for your first day," he said with a welcoming smile. I had met Mark once before in person, and since then, we had spoken several times on the phone. I would quickly come to learn that Mark was not just a great boss and leader for the West Wing, he was also a kindhearted man with a kindred Christian spirit.

I remember encountering Mark just outside the Oval Office ahead of one particularly difficult press conference. Molly, the president's always pleasant and organized assistant and his Oval Office operations coordinator, had had a tree fall on her car minutes before she walked out to leave work. Remarking on the scary turn of events,

Mark talked about God's sovereignty and shared how he had met his wife during high school when he went to take the SAT. As I recall the story, Debbie was "Miss Brandon," having won the town's beauty pageant. Mark courted Debbie as they took their standardized test in the same room. Eventually, the two got married, and, since Mark's car could not drive more than five hundred miles, he borrowed his friend's car to drive to North Carolina for their honeymoon. In an interesting turn of events, Mark ended up running for Congress in that area years later. It was God's sovereign plan.

As Mark talked about God, mere steps from the entryway to the most powerful office in the world, it became clear to me both then and during my time in the Trump White House that Mark Meadows was the real deal. In a crazy "coincidence"—or perhaps not so much—Mark's wife grew up just a few streets away from my hometown church. We shared both common roots and a common faith in Christ. As we navigated the West Wing, my faith—like Mark's—was central.

I also believe that sometimes "coincidence" is not coincidence at all, but rather divine appointment. In addition to sharing wise points on leadership before taking on the job of White House press secretary, my dad also said this to me: "You were made 'for such a time as this.'" The reference was from the book of Esther. Esther, in short, became queen through an unlikely but fortuitous path. As a woman of great character, she was in the right place at the right time, thanks to God's divine appointment. She rose to the occasion as queen and confronted the king, who had murderous plans to annihilate the Jewish people. Her courage saved her people from death. As Esther 4:14 reads, "For if you remain silent at this time, relief and deliverance for the Jews will arise from another place, but you and your father's family will perish. And who knows but that you have come to your royal position for such a time as this?"

Indeed, Esther met the moment, fulfilling God's purpose for her life and setting an example for us all. I took my dad's words to heart. Though coming to my new job amid a global pandemic posed many challenges, maybe I was put in this position "for such a time as this." I know this much—I was certainly meant to hear the story of Esther, if nothing else. Just days after my dad said those words to me, a friend of mine and a Democrat political commentator texted me this: "God has put you in a high place during a time of trouble. You were born for a time 'such as this.'"

Those words are not just applicable to me. I believe God wants everyone to embrace an Esther-like outlook. You are sitting where you are sitting geographically, professionally, and personally for a reason. God wants you to fulfill His purpose. He has great plans and a solemn mission for all of us to further His kingdom. The question is, will you accept it?

CHAPTER 4

THE BRIEFING

"I can do all things through Christ who strengthens me."

—PHILIPPIANS 4:13

On that first day in the White House, the endless hours I had spent meticulously watching the Coronavirus Task Force briefings paid off. I walked into the Oval Office that afternoon, passing the mahogany grandfather clock just to the left of the entryway. I stepped onto the wood floor and then further into the office, crossing the light gold, sunbeam-patterned rug designed during President Reagan's administration. I took a seat on one of the gold and beige couches, just across from the Resolute Desk. The Resolute Desk, crafted from the oak timbers of a British ship and gifted from Queen Victoria in 1880, has an eagle carved on a small front door that opens. Young John F. Kennedy Jr. was famously pictured crawling through this kneehole as his father, President Kennedy, worked. Now, President Trump sat behind the desk, and I sat across from him—my first time in the Oval Office and the first time I would brief the President of the United States ahead of his afternoon briefing.

During that first preparation session, I picked up on how the president liked to prepare. With advisors sitting around him, he flipped open a binder and read through his scripted remarks that he would be reading at the top of his briefing. Using a sharpie, he crossed out certain words and wrote in certain additions. He would pull out some pages from their plastic covers and either cut or fold away portions that he did not like. After reading through his remarks, he would look in the mirror in his private bathroom to quickly freshen up, make a brief stop in Outer Oval (where his assistants sat just outside his office), and then head to the podium. This left little opportunity to go through potential questions. I would come to find that, frequently, the only time left for prepping the president for reporter questions was catching him en route to the briefing room.

During that first prep session, I knew what the dominating question would be. In an interview with CNN, Dr. Fauci told Jake Tapper, "I mean, obviously, you could logically say that…[if] you started mitigation earlier, you could have saved lives."[1] The comment was being spun by reporters to suggest that President Trump didn't act on COVID-19 early enough. The obvious question would be, "Mr. President, did you act early enough? Dr. Fauci, who is standing right beside you, suggested you had not."

I told the president he needed to be prepared, and I reminded him of the timeline.

On January 6th, the CDC had issued a travel notice for Wuhan before there was even a single confirmed case of COVID-19.[2]

On January 11th, when there were still zero cases in the US, the CDC issued a level one travel notice.[3]

On January 17th, still not a single case of coronavirus, but the CDC began public health entry screening at three major US airports.[4]

On January 21st, the CDC activated an emergency operation center with just one case reported in the US.[5]

And then finally, on January 31st—with not a single US COVID death—President Trump issued a travel ban on China.[6] The same ban Joe Biden called "xenophobic."[7]

As a sidenote, this was also the same ban that NPR called "drastic"; *Washington Post* editorials dubbed "a mistake" and a "win—for China"; Vox declared definitively "don't work," and the *New York Times* called "more of an emotional or political reaction," quoting an epidemiologist.[8]

When I finished running through the timeline, President Trump said, "Wow. That's amazing. Go type up that timeline for me."

I ran to my office as quickly as I could, banged away at the keyboard, and returned with a timeline. The president, who rarely carried notes to the podium with him, folded the paper and placed it in his binder. Sure enough, mere minutes into the briefing, he read the timeline word for word.[9]

As I watched the president read my timeline from my new office, I thought, *"Day one in the White House is officially a success."*

DURING MY FIRST FEW weeks on the job, the Coronavirus Task Force, alongside President Trump, gave a few more briefings. I continued to advise the president ahead of the briefings, discovering how I could be most effective in prepping him. In addition to learning his style during those first few weeks, I also learned a valuable second lesson: always bring a backup dress to work.

It was still my first week on the job when I made the foolish decision to wear a dress to work that zipped all the way up the back. My Ted Baker dress was a deep pinkish, burgundy on top, the quarter length sleeves were capped with a navy accent. The bottom of the dress was navy, framing my body and landing just below my knees. Down the back of the dress, from top to bottom was a gold zipper—a gold zipper I would come to regret.

Just before the president's task force briefing, I walked over to the table in my office and bent down to grab a paper on the floor. I heard a small pop and felt the zipper along my back separate. Did my dress just break?! Thankfully, it was still cold out, and I had a coat in my office. I put on my wool coat and walked briskly to the bathroom to survey the damage. My dress was broken—from top to bottom. Now, instead of resembling a dress, it resembled one of those paper robes you get at the doctor. "Leave the opening to the back," the nurse would tell you before changing.

With nothing to change into, I went to the bathroom with a pile of safety pins, doing my best to pin the back of the dress together. It didn't work, and the rather painful safety pins poked me every time I sat down. My only hope was that the president would not summon me. This way, I could wait out the storm in my office and sneak home. Here's to the best laid plans. Shortly after my dress broke, I received a call from one of the president's aides.

"Come down to lower press and talk to the president," they instructed. Lower press was the area just outside the briefing room, where the president stood before heading to the podium.

This was my worst nightmare! My coat, while it provided adequate cover, had a split in the back that opened when I walked. I had no clue how this interaction was going to work. Plus, who wears a coat inside when going to meet the president of the United States?

I snuck out the back door of my office, kept my back to the wall (doing my best Jim Comey impression), and shimmied down to lower press, skirting closely to the wall. In lower press, I found President Trump. I answered his question, my back firmly pressed against the wall in my winter coat. I was certain he thought his new press secretary was crazy! After the briefing, I crossed paths with the president again, this time accompanied by Vice President Pence, Dr. Birx, and Dr. Fauci—my back still glued to the wall. I managed to make it through my dress kerfuffle unscathed, for the most part.

Over the next few weeks, I attended Coronavirus Task Force meetings and continued to advise the president ahead of his briefings. Since these briefings were largely filling the role of the daily briefing with the press secretary, I did not know if I would ever hold a briefing of my own. My predecessor, Stephanie Grisham, had not held a single White House press briefing as press secretary. For over four hundred days, no press secretary had given a briefing. But that changed in an instant.

Out of nowhere, on Wednesday, April 29th, President Trump looked at me and said, "You should do a White House press briefing."

Somewhat surprised at the suggestion, given how long it had been since a press secretary had stood at the podium, I looked at him and said, "I would be happy to do that."

Later in the day, he said it again.

"Kayleigh, you really should do a briefing," a familiar refrain he began to repeat.

I was flattered that he would ask me to give a briefing. It meant that he had faith in me. Beaming at his suggestion, I ran back to my press team and said, "I think the president wants me to do a press briefing. I assume he was being serious when he made the suggestion. Let's start preparing in case."

The president's suggestion came shortly after he had seen a copy of my personal notes. Going through school, I was always a meticulous note taker—never wanting to miss a word of what the professor or lecturer said. I continued this practice in the White House, in taking personal notes for my recollection. President Trump had observed my pages of notes in tiny and neat handwriting.

"Let me see those," he said.

Bemused by my note-taking, he began to solicit my notes in various meetings.

"Hold up those notes. Show the room!" he would say, almost like a proud father wanting the room to recognize my work. I believe the president's observance of my work ethic spurred his decision to call for a briefing.

In my head, I planned to take some time in announcing a formal briefing. I wanted to make the perfect binder and be fully ready for any question thrown my way. This would take significant preparation. A few days or a week perhaps. But after the president made the request several times on Wednesday for me to start briefing, he finally said, "Don't wait until Monday. Do it sooner."

"*What?!*," I thought. "*I have less than forty-eight hours!*" I went back to my team and told them we had a herculean task ahead, and we began making preparations immediately.

The next day, my closest aides and I went into the briefing room to find the proper podium height. Standing behind the podium, White House personnel moved it up and down electronically to find the appropriate leveling.

As I stood there, members of the White House press corps came out of their offices just beyond the briefing room as they curiously observed the adjustments at the lectern. I watched as the reporters continued to file in, crossing the very spot in the back left corner that I had once stood at as an intern in the Bush administration, observing then-White House press secretary Dana Perino. I could hardly believe that in less than twenty-four hours, I would be the one taking the questions.

Before leaving the room, they found the perfect podium measurement—thirty-seven inches high.

"Are you going to be taking the podium soon?" a reporter asked.

"Never say never," I replied.

I returned to my office that Thursday to continue preparation for the next day's briefing.

Julia Hahn, deputy White House communications director, took a first stab at the binder. Under her supervision, her team delivered a roughly forty-page binder. Each page had a bold heading with a topic listed—therapeutics, testing, China, and so on. Beneath the heading were a few top-line talking points. I took the pages she had developed and filled in statistics, quotes, and facts that would substantiate the responses I intended to give. I approached the pages as I would an essay ahead of an Oxford-style tutorial, wanting sourcing and hard facts for every topic. Julia, one of the brightest minds in the entire White House and a brilliant researcher, quickly adapted the binder to my style.

Chad Gilmartin, my principal assistant press secretary, assisted me in research and began to script an opener for me. Chad, my closest aide in the White House, was also smart as a whip. Julia, Chad, and I would strategize for hours, thinking through every possible question that could be asked. Together, we pondered how we could turn a tough question into a good, offensive answer. Meanwhile, my assistant, Lyndee Rose, would prod us to please send the binder so that she could start printing. Undoubtedly a "Type A" personality—totally organized and in command—Lyndee, an assistant who became a close friend, always ensured the black leather binder with the gold, shimmering presidential seal was perfectly tabbed.

Between the four of us, we developed a well-oiled machine. But on the eve of the first briefing, we were just putting the wheels in motion. Chad, Lyndee, and I labored over the binder in my office until after 9:00 p.m. When I got back to my apartment, I studied the binder pages until almost midnight. At 11:15 p.m. that evening, White House Deputy Chief of Staff for Communications Dan Scavino confirmed the press corps' earlier suspicions: ".@PressSec will be at the podium tomorrow afternoon at 2:00pmE," he tweeted, setting off a flurry of interest from reporters.

Heading to sleep just after midnight, I woke up that Friday morning feeling rested. I tried my best to stay calm and confident, listening to a Joyce Meyer sermon on choosing faith over fear as I got ready. I also sent out a tweet, proclaiming what I knew to be true of that moment and every other anxious moment in my life: "'I can do all things through Christ who strengthens me.' – Philippians 4:13." More important than the studying or the physical turning of the pages in my binder was me choosing to turn this seemingly unbelievable moment over to Christ. As a Believer, I knew that while human preparation was important, divine guidance was necessary.

I leaned on that divine guidance as I walked to work that morning, listening to Christian music on the way. Riding down the elevator in my apartment building, I thought how unbelievable it was to be heading to work for my first White House press briefing. This building was the same apartment complex I had lived in as a senior at Georgetown University. I never thought I would be riding the elevator in this capacity.

Arriving at the White House around 7:00 a.m. that morning, I spent hours prepping. At one point, the entire press team huddled in my office and grilled me with questions. We wanted to be ready for every possible scenario. While I practiced for the impending briefing, several past press secretaries reached out with words of encouragement, including one of my recent predecessors, Sarah Sanders. Just before this first briefing, she sent me several pieces of advice, including this: "Most importantly—Pray! Let God carry you through the tough times, give you strength when you don't have any and wisdom to say the right thing." She told me that the last thing she did before every briefing was read her daily devotion from *Jesus Calling*—a practice that I continued before my briefings.

On that first day in May of 2020, Sarah attached her devotional from May 1, 2018—exactly two years prior. The very first words of her *Jesus Calling* devotional from two years ago read, "You are on the path of My choosing. There is no randomness about your life…As you give yourself more and more to a life of constant communion with Me, you will find that you simply have no time to worry."

It was wise advice, and I tried my best to manifest it that day. But my efforts didn't stop the flood of human emotion at 2:00 p.m. Shortly before taking the podium, despite all the preparation, I felt like I was going to cry. I had many years of preparation leading up to this moment. I had climbed the spiral staircases of Oxford University and sparred with esteemed academics who rigorously countered my ideas. I had debated some of the most contentious legal issues of our time at Harvard Law School, and I had heated back and forths on CNN panels, where I was often the only panelist with a conservative viewpoint. But none of those experiences gave me the serenity I sought as I prepared to communicate with the American People on behalf of the US government.

Trying to calm my worries, I got on my knees on the marble floors of the bathroom just outside my office in the West Wing and prayed—something that would become a custom when the going got tough in the White House. I called my mom and dad, who encouraged me and prayed out loud, giving me the peace that I needed. Amid my fears, I knew that it was far more than just my parents and husband who were praying for me. Millions of Christians were too. Their prayers propped me up that day.

After getting those jitters out, I read through the opening script for my briefing one last time and prepared to head into the Oval Office to see President Trump before my briefing. I exited the back door of my office and walked a few steps toward Outer Oval. "You can go into the back," the president's assistant said, referring to the president's private dining area, just beyond the formal Oval Office.

When I got to the back, President Trump was sitting where he always did—at the head of a table, facing a rather large TV. Chief of Staff Mark Meadows, Senior Advisor Jared Kushner, and Vice President Mike Pence were all sitting around the table, beneath the crystal chandelier. Though this was a dining room, President Trump used it as his personal workspace, sifting through papers that quickly covered the dining-table-turned-workspace. I spoke briefly with the group, who encouraged me ahead of my briefing. As I departed from the president's private office, Vice President Pence motioned toward me with praying hands. He told me that he had been praying for me and that he loved my tweet from earlier: "I can do all things through Christ who strengthens me."

I walked back into my office, where my team sat waiting for me to return. "Go time" had finally arrived. The press team exited through the back door of my office, and we all descended past the Secret Service guard, down the ramp, and through a door on the left-hand side that opened up to lower press. So-called "lower press" was the area where mostly younger press staffers sat. These staff members served as the first men and women to interface with the White House press corps on a daily basis. Reporters who wished to speak to me or members of the senior press team would pass through lower press and head up to "upper press," where my office was located.

Now, just after 2:00 p.m., I stood in lower press surrounded by colleagues. In the days leading up to this moment, I had stood in this area along with President Trump and members of the Coronavirus

Task Force before they went out to brief. President Trump would always stand just outside a blue, mechanical sliding door and gaze up at a television just off to the left, which displayed four television networks—Fox News, CNN, MSNBC, and Fox Business. He would look at the empty podium, previewing his impending press conference before bantering with the press staffers and confidently walking to the podium.

Today, it was me standing in this very same spot, looking up at the four television networks. I observed that MSNBC had the shot up of the empty podium, this time previewing my first press briefing. I took a deep breath and looked at Judd Deere, a senior member of the press team who had served under multiple press secretaries. "Are you ready?" he asked. I nodded as he slid the big blue door to the right, revealing an eager White House press corps.

I stepped over the threshold of the door with a smile on my face, as the sound of cameras snapped continually and in unison. Walking past the American flag in my black suit, I finally reached the podium. "Good afternoon," I began before reading an announcement about hospital funding as appropriated in the third round of COVID-19 relief funding. As I spoke, prepared graphics flashed on the screen behind me.

I continued to read my opening remarks, and I was shocked by the peace I felt. I was nearly in tears just before taking the podium, completely overcome with nerves. But now a total serenity, an unexpected confidence filled me. The prayers of so many, the peace that only Jesus Christ can offer had overcome me.

I ended my remarks with a heartwarming video from a White House event earlier in the week. Thanks to a funding program for small businesses, a coffee shop named Bitty & Beau's was able to rehire its employees. Bitty & Beau's hires men and women with intellectual and developmental disabilities, and one of those employees,

Michael Heup, shared this message at the White House: "I love my job, and I'm excited about going back to work…Me and all my amazing co-workers are not broken, and we have lots to offer. I know the great country of the United States isn't broken either."

Following the video of Michael's inspiring words, I shared with the White House press corps that I had spoken with Michael by phone yesterday. He told me that he was writing notes by hand to include with coffee deliveries. He just wanted to put a smile on customers' faces during the early days of the pandemic.

"Bitty and Beau's, they represent the hope and opportunity that is on the horizon for America's workers as their businesses embody the American spirit. Workers, like Michael, show that this country is not broken and that we will recover together," I told the American People. "Michael, thank you. You're an American hero. Thank you for sharing that message of hope.

"And with that, I'll take questions," I concluded.

The closing remarks of my introduction, to me, embody what my goal was each and every time I took to the podium during my tenure as White House press secretary. To fulfill the role of press secretary, it was, of course, my job to convey accurate, clear information to the American public. But I wanted to supplement my duties with something more: I wanted to put a spotlight on Americans whose stories are sometimes lost in reporting that focuses on sensational palace intrigue.

I wanted to highlight the everyday worker doing their job amid a pandemic, the heroic police officers who keep us safe each and every day, the victims of crime in the street—sometimes even children—who tragically lose their lives but rarely gain national attention. My briefings would be a voice for them—the forgotten man, woman, and child. It's why oftentimes at the podium, I would look beyond the press corps and directly into the camera at the American People. I hoped to be their voice.

Highlighting the forgotten man, woman, and child extended beyond the podium. After I began to share the stories of beautiful little toddlers who had fallen victim to crime, one of my assistant press secretaries, Karoline Leavitt, came to me with an idea. "Why don't we get the president to send a letter to the families of these children?" Karoline asked me. I loved the idea, and I asked the president if he would consider it. "Of course," he said. "Let's get it done."

As I remember, one such letter to the family of a sweet young boy read, in part, "While we cannot know God's limitless plans for [your son], we can find peace in knowing that they will be fully realized in the care and comfort of His loving arms. Your beautiful boy's name reminds us of God's promise in Joshua 1:9, 'Be strong and courageous. Do not be afraid; do not be discouraged, for the Lord your God will be with you wherever you go.'"

We tried to locate as many families as we could. Sadly, I was told that some parents were in shelters or unable to be found, but we did our best. I always wondered about the moment these parents received a letter from the president. I remember one day Karoline came in with a smile on her face. "Look at what one of the families posted on social media!" she said. The victim's sister had written, "Today my parents received a priority letter from the White House. They opened it up and it was a letter… signed Donald J. Trump… My baby was truly special. Thank you 45." The post brought so much joy to my heart. This letter could not bring back their little boy, but at least they knew that their president cared.

In the end, I believe I achieved my goal of lifting up the names and stories of Americans often ignored, as I regularly shared the names of forgotten Americans from the White House podium. However, as even my very first briefing would show, some reporters—not all—were intent on editorializing and sowing a narrative rather than earnestly seeking information on behalf of the American People.

To be clear, I have immense respect for both the role of a free press and, on a personal level, for many reporters in the White House press corps. There are indeed men and women who still embody what fair but inquisitive journalism should look like. Even so, there are some whose questions make clear they endeavor for sensationalism over substance.

During my first press briefing, I was asked several very good questions—on the administration's disposition toward China, on oil companies' access to lending facilities, among others. This line of questioning was not only fair but also substantive and of true interest to the American People.

A few questions into the briefing, however, the questioning turned more personal. I was asked: "Will you pledge never to lie to us from that podium?"

Without hesitation, I replied, "I will never lie to you. You have my word on that."

The question, of course, was imbued with an embedded, negative assumption. Of course, I would never lie. How do you get through Oxford, Harvard, and Georgetown without sourcing? Without truthful, well-sourced, well-researched information? More importantly, as a woman of faith, a Christian, and a new mother, telling the truth was in my nature and central to my family life and faith walk. That, however, did not stop some in the press from spinning things wildly out of context, twisting my words, assuming the worst, and engaging in *ad hominem* attacks—like falsely calling me a "liar." In academia, we were taught that personal, *ad hominem* attacks were the last line of defense when you didn't have a winning argument.

As the briefing continued, I maintained my calm, packed my answers with well-vetted and sourced facts, and even managed to navigate those "gotcha" questions like whether Jared Kushner showed a "lack of empathy" in an answer he had given on television and a line of questioning about decades-old, denied sexual assault allegations against President Trump. I do not believe questions of this nature serve the American People, nor do I believe questions like this would be asked of a Democrat administration. I do believe, though, that the American People are smart and wise enough to observe the disparity.

After taking two rounds of questions from the reporters in the room, I ended my first briefing. "Thank you guys so much," I said before closing my binder. "I'm going to cut this short now and go see my little five-month-old here in a few hours."

With that, my first briefing had concluded in what was predictive of the many briefings to come. There would be a mix of substantive questions with sensational ones and oftentimes complete omissions of newsworthy stories that just didn't seem to fit the press narrative. I would be sure to highlight these stories and the men, women, and children affected by them.

As I walked away from the podium, I convened with my staff in lower press. We paused to watch some of the feedback on television and review some of our incoming texts, which were very positive. The first briefing was a team effort, a collaborative endeavor, and one that we celebrated. I walked back to my office and found Dan Scavino sitting on my couch, waiting to congratulate me for a job well done.

As my team exited the room, Chief of Staff Mark Meadows entered. "Not every day will be a great one here," he said. "But this one is. Enjoy it!" The chief of staff then proceeded to say that he had secured a spot for my husband and me to come to dinner with the president at Camp David the next day, an invitation I readily accepted.

Following the briefing, I continued to receive notes, emails, and texts from colleagues in the White House, former co-workers at the campaign and in media, along with friends and family. As I began to read through some of the messages, I realized that the Coronavirus Task Force meeting, led by Vice President Pence, was about to begin in the Situation Room.

I scurried down the stairs, past the White House Mess, and toward the 5,525-square-foot secure conference room operated by the National Security Council. I dropped my phone off at the door, as was required, and entered the room with the task force, eager to aggregate as much information as possible for my next briefing. Still amazed and completely in awe of the role I had been entrusted with, it was not lost upon me that so much history had been made in this very room, including the killing of Osama bin Laden, observed from this conference room.

When I entered the Situation Room, Vice President Pence saw me grabbing a cup of coffee from the corner. He stopped the meeting, looked me in the eye, and said, "Well done," before leading the room in applause. That moment was truly humbling for me. I thanked the vice president and then took my seat along the wall. That afternoon, I left the task force briefing with a bit of pep in my step, knowing that my whole family would be waiting in my office. I had not seen my five-month-old daughter in over three weeks.

"You're not going to recognize her," my husband had texted me the day prior. "She's way different than the last time you saw her," he said, before noting that she had grown into six-to-twelve-month clothing. Ahead of the briefing he sent me a video of her kicking her feet in pink pajamas with gray bunnies. "Tell mommy, 'She can do it,'" you can hear Sean saying in the background.

When I walked in my office, Blake was sitting in her stroller with her feet propped up on the bar. Sean was right. She was so much bigger. In fact, she looked like an entirely different baby! I hugged her and my family, and then we all walked down that same slope toward lower press I had walked down earlier before my briefing. This time, though, I walked with my family through the glass-paned doors and out onto the iconic West Colonnade.

The West Colonnade is the outdoor pathway between the West Wing and the Executive Residence. Lined with bright white columns, the president would regularly walk the path with senior staff or guests. As my family and I walked along the colonnade, I recounted for them a story they had surely already heard but may have forgotten.

I reminded my family that just over a decade ago, when I was a White House intern, I had traversed the colonnade with Giants quarterback Eli Manning. At the time, I was beside myself with excitement when my supervisor asked me to walk Eli from the Super Bowl XLII championship celebration on the South Lawn to the West Wing Lobby. The staff knew that I was a big fan of the Manning brothers, though more specifically Peyton Manning. Nevertheless, they gave me the honor of escorting Eli. The task meant that I would have just under a minute to make small talk. After all, the West Colonnade that we would walk along was also dubbed the "45-second commute," as it took roughly forty-five seconds to walk along the path.[10]

After carefully planning my black suit and shiny red shirt in my Georgetown dorm, I came up with the brilliant idea of bringing my Peyton Manning Colts jersey with me to the White House that day. It was the same jersey I wore to the very rainy Super Bowl XLI with my dad the year prior in Miami, Florida, where we watched Peyton Manning and Tony Dungy win their very first Super Bowl victory.

"Why not ask Eli to sign Peyton's jersey?" I thought. *"He'd probably be honored. Nothing could go wrong."*

The next day, I asked Eli to sign the jersey, just as I had planned. He gave me a bit of a confused expression before kindly obliging to sign the jersey. "Eli" he scribbled in cursive, atop the "1" in the "18" on the back of Peyton's jersey.

Very proud of my accomplishment, I thought, "*Hmm…maybe I should take this a step further and ask for a picture.*" We were waiting for Eli to be escorted back to President Bush, so we had time. I saw an older man in the corner, and settled on my plan, "*This is my moment!*"

"Eli, would you mind if I got a picture?" I asked. He said sure, and then I turned to the older gentleman, "Would you mind taking this?"

I got my picture, gratified by all that I had achieved that day as a young intern. As the Giants team members were escorted back to the president, a staffer said to me, "Kayleigh, do you know what you just did?!"

"What?" I replied, puzzled by the tone.

"You just asked Tom Coughlin, the HEAD COACH of the Giants, to take YOUR picture!"

At the time, I was horrified at my blunder.

Now, walking along the West Colonnade with my family after my very first White House press briefing, I was laughing at the younger version of myself.

At the end of the colonnade, my family and I took a right and walked toward the South Lawn. We stood behind by the White House reporters, there to photograph President Trump and ask him questions as he walked across the lawn toward Marine One—the famous green and white helicopter, operated by the United States Marine Corps. Marine One was typically the mode of transportation to carry the president from the White House lawn to Joint Base

Andrews (JBA), a US Air Force base from which Air Force One takes off.

In this case, Marine One was not taking off for JBA but instead for Camp David, the well-known presidential getaway. This was the first time President Trump would be leaving the White House in over a month.[11] Though he traveled regularly as president, he had been in the White House for an extended period of time due to the onset of the COVID-19 pandemic. Camp David would be his first time out of DC in quite some time.

As President Trump prepared to exit the White House, Secret Service asked me to stay back and sit on a bench with Blake because of the intensity of a Marine One takeoff. It was our first time observing Marine One depart from the White House lawn, and we weren't prepared for the gusts of wind that the helicopter's blades would produce. Blake and I sat on a bench just off the colonnade, and Fox News's John Roberts stopped to say hello. To this day, I call it Blake's first White House "gaggle"—a term used for an informal question and answer period with reporters.

Blake would soon be known as "Baby Blake" around the White House. Her smiling face would be a frequent scene in the building as she came to visit Mommy. "Baby Blake!" a kind Secret Service officer shouted from behind the desk during one of her visits with my mom and sister. "I don't know you all, but I know Baby Blake, so you're good!" he laughed.

Sitting on that bench with my daughter and watching President Trump board Marine One from afar, I had no idea what my White House future would hold. If a global pandemic was not enough, the nation would endure months of violent protest, the leader of the free world getting coronavirus, and so much more in the months that followed. And I had a front row seat to it all.

CHAPTER 5

OFFENSE ONLY

"The opposite for courage is not cowardice, it is
conformity. Even a dead fish can go with the flow."

—Rollo May, later cited and expounded upon
by Jim Hightower to produce this rendition[1]

My dad, Mike McEnany, is a natural born leader. I saw it growing up, and I admired it. His father, Pat McEnany, died when he was just six years old. Raised by a single, working mom, my dad grew up quick, learning to take the city bus as a young first grader through the crowded streets of Miami, Florida. But his struggles built character and instilled a fight within him. At six feet tall, my dad was small for the position of defensive end, but football was his passion, and he was determined to pursue it. He walked on to the Mississippi State Bulldogs football team, and, after earning a scholarship, his determination managed to get him one of the top sacks records at the university. There was no doubt that Mike McEnany had "the eye of the tiger."

During his time on MSU's football team, his leadership did not go unnoticed. By his senior year, he was named captain of the team, a position he excelled at. When football ended, he rechanneled that energy and, despite starting with little, he built a commercial roofing company from the ground up. More important, though, than achieving worldly success, my dad is beloved by those who work for him. I wanted to learn how to lead like that.

As I prepared to take my new job at the White House, I knew that I would be leading a press team. Roughly a dozen men and women would ultimately work for me, and I wanted to be more than just a boss. I endeavored to be a leader who would inspire, someone my team could look up to. In short, I hoped to be like my dad. Up to this point, I had never managed a team of individuals, so I looked to my dad for advice.

Ahead of my trip up to DC, my dad had written out quotes and recommendations on leadership. "Leadership is the capacity and will to rally men and women to a common purpose and the character which inspires confidence," read one quote from Field Marshal Bernard Montgomery, one of the most accomplished British commanders in World War II. My dad encouraged me to (1) identify the common purpose of our press shop; (2) articulate it so that everyone knows that purpose; (3) write it down and post it in the office; and (4) make every decision with that common purpose in mind—the "goal line" we must cross to win.

During my long truck ride up the eastern corridor, I gave a lot of thought to what this motto should be. Then, it dawned on me: "Offense Only." In my mind, it was the absolute, perfect motto. For years, I had seen a barrage of negative, slanted news stories—not just about President Trump—but about Republicans and conservatives generally. The liberal media seemed to have a preconceived viewpoint that always left Republicans on the losing end of a story. I wanted to change that, and we would do it by being on offense.

In practice, this meant something very specific. If a press inquiry came in filled with anonymous leaks and sensationalism, speculating about supposed conversations in a private meeting and so-called "palace intrigue," we weren't going to spend the entire day on it. Sure, someone in the press shop would respond, but we wouldn't let the media drive the narrative. We would keep the focus on the administration priorities—be it Operation Legend, which protected children in vulnerable communities and held criminals accountable, or Operation Warp Speed, which secured hundreds of millions of vaccines to defeat COVID-19.

"Offense Only" was perfect.

Prior to starting the job, I thought a lot about my relationship with the press. I wanted to have a good working relationship. Shortly after beginning as White House press secretary, I met with the head of the White House Correspondents' Association, Jon Karl, and several of his colleagues on the board of the association. I wanted to start off on the right foot.

Jon was presumably interested in fostering a productive relationship between the new press secretary and the press corps, as we had exchanged amicable texts ahead of our first in-person interaction. It was a collegial meeting, where we discussed how to facilitate the press secretary-press interaction. But the meeting ended a bit curiously. At the end of the meeting, Jon handed me a copy of his book entitled *Front Row at the Trump Show*. Rather than covering an administration elected by the American People, it appeared—at least from the title of the book—Jon thought he was starring in a "show" from which he could write a book.

Still, I was prepared to give the relationship an opportunity. At the same time, however, I was not going to be Pollyanna. I had watched how the press treated the Trump administration, and I would not be railroaded or steamrolled. I would be prepared in the event that members of the press corps asked "gotcha" questions. Should that moment come, I would be ready.

It didn't take long for the press to pursue this line of questioning. Indeed, as I mentioned earlier, there were a few questions of this nature in my first briefing. My second White House press briefing, however, is where I made the determination that I would have to hold the press accountable. For me, the red line was if the press decided to attack me personally. These briefings were not supposed to be about me. They were about transmitting information to the American public. Should they veer from that purpose, I would be ready to respond.

The "gotcha" question that came was the final one of my second briefing, and it went like this: "Kayleigh, in a previous life, before you were press secretary, you worked for the campaign. And you made a comment, I believe, on Fox, in which you said, 'President Trump will not allow the coronavirus to come to this country.' Given what has happened since then, obviously, would you like to take that back?"[2]

Notably, just about a week before I made this remark, none other than Dr. Anthony Fauci, a hero of the media and the left, said that the risk of coronavirus to the United States was "just minuscule"— of course a fact left out of the reporter's question.[3]

I responded to the reporter by first adding context left out of the question. During that Fox appearance, I had been asked about President Trump's travel restrictions, and I was noting the intent behind those restrictions, which was: "We will not see the coronavirus come here." In that same appearance, I had said, "We will not see terrorism come here," in a reference to the president's earlier set of travel restrictions.

By way of comparison, as one social media user noted, it is similar to an athlete saying, "I will win this race." Indeed, it is his intent to win the race. Should he not prevail, should he be called a liar for stating his intent to win a race that had not yet occurred? That would obviously be absurd!

After giving an explanation to the reporter, I took it a step further: "I guess I would turn the question back on the media, and ask similar questions:

"Does *Vox* want to take back that they proclaimed that the coronavirus would not be a deadly pandemic?[4]

"Does the *Washington Post* want to take back that they told Americans to 'Get a grippe… the flu is bigger than coronavirus'?[5]

"Does the *Washington Post*, likewise, want to take back that 'our brains are causing us to exaggerate the threat of the coronavirus'?[6]

"Does the *New York Times* want to take back that fear of the virus may be spreading faster than the virus itself?[7]

"Does NPR want to take back that the flu was a much bigger threat than the coronavirus?[8]

"And finally, once again, the *Washington Post*—would they like to take back that the government should not respond aggressively to the coronavirus?[9]

"I'll leave you with those questions and maybe you'll have some answers in a few days," I ended before walking away from the podium, off the riser, and back into lower press.[10]

In somewhat of a coincidence, I had reviewed those media headlines at the very last minute just before heading to the podium. Thank goodness! I was prepared for the moment, ready to fact check the media's coverage if they tried to attack me personally. It's a moment that I hoped would never happen. I don't believe personal, scathing questions are productive or are what the American People want to see.

It's hard to envision a scenario where President Biden's White House press secretary, Jen Psaki, would be asked such a personal question. Early in the administration, old tweets surfaced from the current press secretary, where she called Senator Lindsey Graham— "LadyG"—in what was widely labeled a homophobic insult.[11] Psaki was not asked about this from the podium.[12] One can only imagine if our roles were reversed.

The truth of the matter is—there is one standard of questioning for a Republican administration and an entirely different standard for a Democrat one. Don't take it from me. Look for yourself at some of the questions Jen Psaki has fielded.

"[C]ould you just give us some color about what it was like for him going into the Oval Office? He's been waiting for this for so long. What was his reaction?" asked one enterprising reporter during Psaki's first briefing.[13]

"[W]ill he keep Donald Trump's Air Force One color scheme change?" asked another.[14]

"[C]an you clarify for us what happened with the President's dogs? There's some reports that one of them was involved in a biting incident."[15]

Yes, they asked about the dog. And the cat…

"Just quickly, a little update on the White House cat[?]"[16]

Truly probing questions from an inquisitive press corps. Rewind a few months earlier and the White House press corps opted to take on an entirely different tone as I stood behind the podium as a part of a Republican administration.

"Let me ask, if I can, Kayleigh: Why does the president keep hiring people who are 'dumb as a rock,' 'overrated,' 'way over their heads,' 'wacko,' and 'incompetent'?" I was asked.[17]

"So, you've used the phrase 'warriors' to describe everyday Americans [fighting the pandemic]. The president is using that phrase as well. What's the thinking behind using that description? And is that basically asking Americans to put themselves in harm's way—harm's way like warriors do?" another reporter inquired.[18] As if the president praising the American People, who were valiantly fighting COVID-19, was somehow a call to arms.

"[D]oes President Trump believe that it was a good thing that the South lost the Civil War?"[19] Yes, that was actually a question. So stunned by the question, I stopped in my tracks, ceased flipping the pages of my binder, and looked up at the reporter in pure bewilderment.[20] "[Y]our first question is absolutely absurd. He's proud of the *United* States of America," I replied. I learned the hard way that there is, indeed, such a thing as a dumb question.

In addition to the disparity in questions, there are also different standards in reporting between Republican and Democrat administrations. When a glowing *Glamour* profile came out about women in the Joe Biden campaign, Maggie Haberman of the *New York Times* tweeted: "Putting aside everything else, it is rare to hear a woman speaking unapologetically and unselfconsciously about life having kids and an intense job...."

What?!

Where had Maggie been for the entirety of the Trump presidency?

Sarah Huckabee Sanders was the first mom to become White House press secretary.

I was the first mom to an infant to become press secretary.

Plus, there were countless women in the Trump administration and campaign who regularly spoke "about life having kids and an intense job." Kellyanne Conway, Lara Trump, Mercedes Schlapp, Katrina Pierson to name just a few.

Maggie knew this all too well. In fact, when I was with the Trump campaign, the *New York Times* had agreed to do a story on women in the Trump campaign. Maggie and her colleague came to the Republican National Committee annex in Virginia and took pictures of the senior female staff on the Trump campaign. Lara Trump and I were pregnant at the time. We sat in the main conference room with Maggie, as the women of the Trump campaign spoke "unapologetically and unselfconsciously" to use Maggie's words. Unsurprisingly, none of that made it into the piece. The pictures that they had taken were sidelined, and the article was little more than a bland account of President Trump's challenges with female voters.[21]

Maggie's tweet about the mothers on the Biden campaign prompted me to send a pretty straightforward response back on Twitter. I simply posted a picture of me pushing my newborn daughter in a stroller through the White House after a long day's work.[22]

Her response? "This is the most extensive response I've had from the taxpayer-funded press secretary in months, on any topic."[23]

Interestingly, she failed to mention that one of my top deputies, Judd Deere, responded to all of her inquiries—a routine act of delegation in a White House press shop. Moreover, another left-out nugget of truth: Beyond my deputy answering her inquiries, the last time she had reached out to me—with one exception—was six months prior to sending her tweet. The real issue is that I would not be an anonymous source for her. When that became clear, the outreach ceased.

The disparity in questioning and the difference in coverage is a reflection of the press's disposition at large. Any casual observer can see the media's liberal bias. They hardly conceal it these days. But in case you need to be convinced, the bias is quantifiable.

Harvard Kennedy School published a report on the media's coverage of President Trump's first one hundred days in office. CNN and NBC both had 93 percent negative coverage of President Trump. The *New York Times* was 87 percent negative, and the *Washington Post* 83 percent negative. The list went on with the study ultimately concluding: "Trump has received unsparing coverage for most weeks of his presidency, without a single major topic where Trump's coverage, on balance, was more positive than negative, setting a new standard for unfavorable press coverage of a president."[24]

The American public recognizes this skew. Midway through President Trump's term, an Axios/SurveyMonkey poll found that a full 92 percent of Republicans thought "news sources report news they know to be fake, false or purposely misleading" either "a lot" or "some" of the time.[25] Seventy-nine percent of independents agreed with that proposition. The level of trust has fallen so low that the 2021 Edelman Trust Barometer found that "[f]or the first time ever, fewer than half of all Americans have trust in traditional media," as reported by Axios.[26] Further, echoing its 2018 poll, Axios noted in January of 2021 that "56 percent of Americans agree with the statement that 'Journalists and reporters are purposely trying to mislead people by saying things they know are false or gross exaggerations.'"[27] Perhaps even more alarming, in a Reuters Institute survey of forty-six countries, the United States finished "dead last" in media trust.[28]

I don't need a trust barometer, a survey, or a poll to tell me this, though, because I lived it on the sets of CNN throughout the 2016 election. Panels were stacked eight to one, liberal to conservative—sometimes seven to two if you were lucky. Democrat presidential nominee Hillary Clinton's email scandal was largely ignored in favor of incessant, breathless coverage of any accusations or negative story against soon-to-be President Trump. The bias was systemic and pervasive, not just at CNN but across many media outlets. As conservatives, we had to expose it and fight back.

⚬⚬⚬

FIGHTING BACK AGAINST THE behemoth liberal media, however, comes with a price. As an institution, the media holds quite a large megaphone, and make no mistake, they will repurpose it to target Republicans or critics. We saw it when *60 Minutes* manufactured a COVID-19 scandal against Florida governor Ron DeSantis, while ignoring the very real scandal against New York governor Andrew Cuomo.[29] We saw it when the *Washington Post* decided to "fact check" South Carolina senator Tim Scott's ancestry while ignoring plagiarism accusations against Vice President Kamala Harris.[30] And I certainly saw it, on a personal level, when I began to challenge the media.

Maggie Haberman decided it was newsworthy to target my press briefings in the pages of her paper, noting that it was "increasingly unclear what purpose" they served. That was a curious remark given that I had told her face-to-face the purpose they served. Prior to the piece coming out, I had spoken to her on Air Force One, knowing that she had an upcoming hit piece on my briefings. During our conversation, Maggie asked me the purpose of my briefings and what I thought they accomplished. I explained that I was providing information on behalf of the president, and that I thought my briefings accomplished quite a lot. For example, my briefings brought attention to stories that were oftentimes neglected by reporters, like when I highlighted children dying in the streets of Chicago and officers who lost their lives in the line of duty.

In fact, just a few weeks earlier, I had ended a July briefing this way: "This is our last press briefing of the week, and so I just wanted to make a plea for peace in our streets because far too many children have been lost. It's important to know their names. It's important to see their faces. And may we all hold in our prayers and keep close to our hearts the families of Natalia Wallace, who was seven; Mekhi James, who was three; Vernado Jones Jr., who was fourteen; Sincere Gaston, who was one; Lena Nunez, who was ten; Amaria Jones, who was thirteen; Davon McNeal, who was eleven; and Secoriea Turner, down in Atlanta, who was eight."

"Their names matter," I told Maggie, recalling briefing moments like this.

"Can I use that in my story?" she asked me.

I obliged. Unsurprisingly, that detail never made it into the story.

Instead, the story seemed to lament my preparation: "Ms. McEnany and members of the White House communications staff spend much of the mornings on the days she briefs in preparation for her to take the podium, assembling talking points and counterattacks that are then stuffed into an oversized binder."[31]

For the layman, this is called hard work and preparation. For a liberal *New York Times* reporter, this is something to bemoan.

As for the "oversized binder," that become a subject of interest not just for the *New York Times* but for other outlets as well. After a camera in the briefing room caught a picture of the tabs in my binder, CNN published an article entitled "Decoding the mysteries of Kayleigh McEnany's briefing book," wherein the CNN editor-at-large speculated what was in each of my tabs.[32] "So organized!" read the *Washington Post* headline after the picture of my tabs emerged. The *Post's* article contained a quote from an editor who had covered ten presidents. "[M]ost press secretaries routinely come to the podium armed with talking points, opening statements and comebacks for likely questions given the topics of the moment," the editor said. "But Kayleigh arrives with the War and Peace of briefing materials. In more than 52 years of covering briefings…I've never seen a binder that prodigious at a regular briefing."[33]

I'll take it!

To be fair, Julia did her best to keep the binder much slimmer than the renowned nearly six-hundred-thousand-word novel, *War and Peace*. Julia and I would debate whether we could cut out a certain page—Julia fighting to remove it, me fighting to keep it. Julia was looking out for my best interests. There was nothing worse than having to flip through too many pages, as I scavenged what grew to be sometimes a 150-page binder.

Maggie's *New York Times* hit piece came around the same time as another piece on my briefings, but this one from Andrew Malcolm. Malcolm got at the heart of what was so problematic in the briefing room during Trump's tenure: "A few reporters sought – and got – fame or notoriety by virtue-signaling to liberals their opposition to Trump's presidency…." He wrote. "But McEnany is not bothered or conflicted about the job demands of Trump press secretary. No need to court, coddle or assuage a hostile White House press corps."[34]

He was exactly right.

For reporters, part of seeking "fame or notoriety" was ensuring they received a steady stream of leaks from inside the West Wing. Those of us who refused to leak what happened in an Oval Office meeting or in personal conversations with the president often received the worst press coverage. That was one of the problems I found in Washington—people who cared more about what the *New York Times* or *Washington Post* wrote about them versus what the American People needed from them. In the Trump administration, for the most part, we had tireless public servants willing to break from the mold of caring what the media elite said about them, instead focusing on things like Middle East peace and a roaring, but accessible, economy with opportunity for all. Nevertheless, there were some who knew information was currency in Washington—currency they used with fame-seeking reporters.

I, for one, refused to be an actor in the "show" Jon Karl described on the cover of the book that he handed me. Because I would not play the part—ahead of his next book deal—Jon went into attack mode. He authored a piece about me in the blatantly partisan

Washington Post, lamenting "the most troubling moment[s]" of my briefing. What was so troubling to Jonathan Karl? The fact that I challenged the press and questioned their preoccupation with topics they felt were unfavorable to President Trump at the expense of very important topics like children dying in the streets.

"The most troubling moment that day came as McEnany ended the briefing," Jon wrote. I had ended my briefing in a manner similar to how I began it. At the start of my briefing, I spoke about the misguided "defund the police" movement and pointed out that—over the July Fourth holiday weekend alone—"in New York, there were forty-four shootings with eleven killed; in Chicago, seventy-five people were shot with thirteen killed; and, tragically, at least five of these individuals were children who were killed in cities across the country."[35] I then highlighted a beautiful line from the president's Fourth of July speech. The president had said, "Never forget: We are one family and one nation.... We will teach our children to cherish and adore their country so...they can build its future." I then proceeded to take questions.

The first question: "Why is the president so supportive of flying the Confederate flag?"

"The president never said that," I pointed out. "Again, you're taking his tweet completely out of context."

The probing from reporters continued: "Does he think it was a mistake for NASCAR to ban it?"

"Has he considered banning the Confederate flag from Trump rallies?"

All non-official merchandise was already banned from Trump rallies, Confederate flags included. The line of questioning on the Confederate flag persisted the entirety of the briefing, prompting me to end the briefing this way: "I was asked probably twelve questions about the Confederate flag. This president is focused on action, and

I'm a little dismayed that I didn't receive one question on the deaths that we got in this country this weekend. I didn't receive one question about New York City shootings doubling for the third straight week. And over the last seven days, shootings skyrocketed by 142 percent. Not one question. I didn't receive one question about five children who were killed.

"And I'll leave you with this remark by a dad—it broke my heart—a dad of an eight-year-old lost in Atlanta this weekend: 'They say black lives matter…you killed a child. She didn't do nothing to nobody,' was his quote. We need to be focused on securing our streets, making sure no lives are lost because all black lives matter—that of David Dorn and that of this eight-year-old girl."

This was "the most troubling moment" of my briefing for Jon Karl?

Wow.

The administration's focus on crime in the streets also angered Democrat elected officials. Like when I called out Chicago mayor Lori Lightfoot from the podium: "[B]lack men and women…die of homicide at eight times greater [a rate] than that of white individuals and Hispanic individuals combined…. So that's an extraordinary thing that we want to look at. I've listed for you the names of these kids who have died across this country. It is unacceptable, and under this president, he'll take action. And the derelict mayor of Chicago should step up and ask for federal help because she's doing a very poor job at securing her streets."[36]

Apparently triggered by the fact that I had exposed a crushing problem in her city, Mayor Lightfoot replied with a tweet: "Hey, Karen. Watch your mouth."[37] As the New York Post pointed out, "Karen" was "social media shorthand for an entitled, meddling, typically middle-aged white woman."[38] The Mayor of Chicago could call me whatever she liked. My focus was on the bloodshed occurring far too often in her city and many others.

Jon Karl went on to explain his problem with me highlighting crime in the streets by saying this, "Rising crime rates are an important issue, but the administration wasn't offering any new policy to address it...."

Well, the White House did announce a new policy two days later, called Operation Legend. The operation was named after four-year-old LeGend Taliferro, who was shot and killed in Kansas City as he peacefully slept in his bed. By facilitating cooperation between federal and local law enforcement, Operation Legend succeeded in making six thousand arrests, including 467 homicide arrests.[39] Not only that, Operation Legend actually found the suspected murderer of LeGend. I remember that day—August 13, 2020—when I received a call from Kerri Kupec, director of communications and public affairs at the Department of Justice.

"Kayleigh, we found the suspect in LeGend's killing," she said with urgency in her voice.

"I can't believe it. That's great news!" I said, rushing back to my office, preparing to share the development with the president.

I printed a picture of little LeGend, wearing a red cape and a shirt featuring a blue and red ribbon heart on it. In the center of the heart were the letters "CHD," standing for "congenital heart defect." On the blue portion of the heart read the words "Born with a broken heart." LeGend had undergone open heart surgery at five months old to treat his rare congenital heart defect. He had survived the surgery only to be senselessly murdered at the young age of four.

I went to Outer Oval with the picture and said that I needed to see the president immediately. I walked in to find him alone at the Resolute Desk. "Mr. President," I told him. "The DOJ found the suspect in LeGend Taliferro's murder." I showed him the picture of this sweet little boy; he took it and rejoiced at the news.

A few minutes later the president took to the White House podium and made the announcement: "Hello, everyone. Thank you very much. It was just announced by Attorney General Barr that they've caught the killer of LeGend Taliferro—horribly shot—a young man, wonderful young man," he said, holding up the picture of LeGend that I had printed for him. "As you know, we named Operation LeGend after LeGend Taliferro, where we're going to be helping out, and are in the process of helping out, cities throughout our country that have difficulty with crime—in particular, certain types of crime. So that's really good news. They caught the killer of LeGend."[40]

Despite announcing this new operation and the successful results that followed, I do not recall being asked a single question about it—and definitely not one from Jon Karl. This is the kind of meaningful work that the White House press corps rarely, if ever, asked about, but it was important to the American People.

Jon Karl accused me of "violating public trust," when in reality, by holding the press accountable, I was trying to reestablish "public trust" between the press and the People. Karl wrote that the job of a press secretary was "to inform the public: to be an intermediary between the president and a press corps the public relies on for information." I did that each and every day. Ahead of a briefing, I went to great lengths to ensure that I knew where the president stood on every conceivable topic that could come up. My regular access to President Trump made that much easier. I could hardly go one morning without fielding a call from my boss before 8:00 a.m. I was regularly summoned to the Oval Office for the president to update me on his thinking and always got access to him, no matter the day's schedule and especially before briefings. I was thankful for it. It made me a better press secretary. After all, I was speaking for the president of the United States, not myself.

During my briefings and in private conversations with reporters, I brought regular updates on the president's thinking and the administration's work more broadly. Personally calling secretaries of departments and heads of agencies, I gathered numbers, facts, and statistics on the topics of the day. From COVID-19 updates and the status of unemployment benefits to Middle East peace deals and China's human rights atrocities against the Uighurs, I provided an abundance of information to a press often more interested in Confederate flags and insider gossip.

On a daily basis, I "inform[ed] the public" as an "intermediary between the president and a press corps," to use Karl's words. But as for the press and their duty to provide "information… the public relies on," as Karl also described….

Well…about that. The months following the Trump administration would expose just how "reliable" the information coming from the American press actually was.

CHAPTER 6

VINDICATION

"A lie doesn't become truth, wrong doesn't become right,
and evil doesn't become good, just because it's accepted
by a majority."

—BOOKER T. WASHINGTON

Since I left the White House, there has been a whole lot of vindication. As it turns out, the press was wrong, and Trump was right on a whole host of issues. We now know that there was not verified intelligence detailing Russian bounties on the heads of US soldiers. We know that President Trump was correct in raising the possibility that the Wuhan Institute of Virology might have been the origin of COVID-19. And we know that the press was wrong in reporting "Protesters Dispersed With Tear Gas So Trump Could Pose at Church."[1] I told the White House press corps all of these facts from the podium, but it didn't stop them from running with the false reporting.

While there have been countless examples of erroneous reporting (now exposed), there has been very little accountability. No journalist lost their job. Very few corrections have been issued. There has not been a public reckoning by a major publication or outlet, apologizing for having misled their readers or viewers. No, there has just been silence. There has been silence and projection, as the press—ignoring its own lies—instead projects the label of "liar" onto others.

Completely disregarding their own track record, the press attacks Republicans with *ad hominem* smears—liar, racist, misogynist. For press secretaries, they tend to go with the "liar" moniker. They rely on so-called "fact"-checkers to make their case. These "fact"-checkers are little more than arms of the Democrat party, housed within left-wing outlets like the *Washington Post* and PolitiFact. Just a cursory glance at these "fact"-checks will tell you all you need to know about their credibility.

A 2013 study of some of these "fact"-checkers found that Republicans are labeled dishonest at three times the rate of Democrats.[2] "Fact" checking in the Trump era was no different. Tim Graham pointed out that, "Overall, from the start of 2019 through August 2020, Trump has gotten 197 Truth-O-Meter ratings, and Biden has only gotten 64," with PolitiFact choosing to fact check the Republican president far more often than his Democrat opponent.[3] It should come as no surprise that 79 percent of Trump's ratings were "Mostly False or worse" while just 45 percent of Biden's garnered the same designation.[4] Interestingly, during this time period, we now know that Biden and the lapdog media deserved far more "Mostly False or worse" designations.

As the "fact"-checkers were skewering President Trump, the media was telling us that Russia had bounties on the heads of US soldiers, and Trump was doing nothing about it. Using this story, Biden accused President Trump of "betrayal."

Fact check ten months later: *FALSE.*

Also during this time, the media claimed President Trump gassed innocent protesters to clear the way for him to have a photo op at

St. John's Church holding a Bible. Joe Biden, Kamala Harris, and Nancy Pelosi all seized on the story.

Fact check one year later: *FALSE*.

The media was also telling the world that the Hunter Biden laptop story, containing damning details was mere "Russian disinformation." Biden, unsurprisingly, picked up the talking point as well.

Fact check one year later: *FALSE*.

Where were the fact-checks on these stories in real time? The sad truth is that the "fact"-checkers simply were not interested in dinging the Democrat nominee during a presidential election. As Dr. Edwin J. Feulner accurately observed, the "fact"-checking—when placed under scrutiny—begins to look more like "opinion-checking."[5] He goes on to pose this question: "Who checks the fact-checkers?" The next logical question becomes, "Who fact-checks the media?" The answer is no one. I would be remiss if I did not use at least a small portion of this book to compile just a handful of the stories that the media got so wrong.

Russian Bounties

On June 26, 2020, the *New York Times* published an explosive report: "Russia Secretly Offered Afghan Militants Bounties to Kill U.S. Troops, Intelligence Says" followed by a sub-heading, "The Trump administration has been deliberating for months about what to do about a stunning intelligence assessment."[6]

The article, based on anonymous sources (of course), asserted that President Trump had been briefed about these supposed Russian bounties, that the intelligence was conclusive, and that President Trump had failed to take action on the matter.

The article was an outright falsehood.

First, President Trump had never been briefed on the matter. Second, the intelligence was not verified. But that didn't stop then-Democrat presidential nominee Joe Biden from accusing Trump of "betrayal of the most sacred duty we bear as a nation – to protect and equip our troops when we send them into harm's way."[7]

The press, for their part, asked dozens and dozens of questions about it for many weeks thereafter. I told the White House press corps repeatedly that the intelligence was "not verified"; that there was "no consensus in the intelligence community"; and that there were in fact "dissenting views" on the matter. I warned them that this would impinge on our ability to collect intelligence in the future. "Who's going to want to cooperate with the United States intelligence community…Which allies will want to share information with us if they know that some rogue intelligence officer can go splash that information on the front page of a major US newspaper?" I asked before reading statements from the CIA, the National Security Council, and the Office of the Director of National Intelligence detailing that point.

But the questioning and speculation continued. "There have been reports that some American service members actually were killed as a result of this Russian bounty. What information do you have on that?" one reporter asked.[8]

The question was based on the *New York Times* erroneously linking the deaths of servicemen with the Russian bounties. "The debate over Russian bounties has brought the deaths of Staff Sgt. Christopher Slutman, 43, Sgt. Robert A. Hendriks, 25, and Staff Sgt. Benjamin Hines, 31, to the forefront of American consciousness after 18 years of U.S. involvement in Afghanistan," the *Times* reported.[9] The so-called "paper of record" even solicited quotes from the families, who rightfully noted, if true, it would be heartbreaking.[10] I cannot imagine the pain of a Gold Star family, reading in the

Times that their commander-in-chief failed to act, and their son or daughter might have perished due to this inaction.

As we would learn ten months later, the story was not true.

I cautioned reporters from the podium: "Before buying into…a narrative from the *New York Times* that falsely states something about the president…wait for the facts to come out."

But wait they did not.

For those who did not take me and the administration at our word, they learned of the falsehood of the bounty story when the left-wing *Daily Beast* reported, "US Intel Walks Back Claim Russians Put Bounties on American Troops" followed by, "It was a huge election-time story that prompted cries of treason. But according to a newly disclosed assessment, Donald Trump might have been right to call it a 'hoax.'"[11] This assessment from the Biden administration confirmed that there was "low to moderate" confidence in the intelligence on Russian bounties. In other words, the intelligence was not conclusive, and the egregious headlines asserting otherwise for ten months were false.

Stunning. Absolutely stunning. The anonymous sourcing was wrong, and the *New York Times'* false reporting could very likely have influenced the election.

Interestingly, the same publication that published the Russia bounty story took a far different approach when reporting on John Kerry, currently serving as first United States Special Presidential Envoy for Climate. The *Times* reported that Kerry had, alarmingly, notified a state sponsor of terrorism (Iran) about covert intelligence regarding Israel (our ally). He had reportedly shared that Israel had waged attacks in Syria at least two hundred times. Instead of making it the headline, though, the *Times* buried the allegation in paragraph twenty-two of a twenty-six-paragraph story.[12]

For President Trump, however, headline-inducing leaks were a near constant in his administration. As I shared in one briefing, "According to the DOJ, classified leaks surged in this administration. There were, under President Obama, just thirty-nine, on average, criminal leak referrals. In this administration, we've seen one hundred criminal leak referrals to the DOJ in 2017, eighty-eight in 2018, and one hundred and four on average per year."[13] Those leaks made the job all that much harder. Phone calls with foreign leaders, meetings with government officials, reports of alleged intelligence— all spilled across the front pages of newspapers. It was infuriating, prompting me to say: "To the anonymous sources who leak classified information, you should know this: you may seek to undermine our president, but in fact, you undermine our country's safety and our country's security."[14]

The Wuhan Institute of Virology

The day before my first press briefing, President Trump was asked, "Have you seen anything at this point that gives you a high degree of confidence that the Wuhan Institute of Virology was the origin of the virus?"

"Yes, I have. Yes, I have," he answered. "And I think the World Health Organization should be ashamed of themselves because they're like the public relations agency for China."[15]

Now, in hindsight, it appears the press corps was China's public relations agency as well. The press derided Trump for suggesting the virus originated in a lab in China rather than originating naturally from a bat. NPR claimed that the lab leak theory had been "debunked."[16] The *New York Times* called the lab leak claim a "fringe theory."[17] The *Washington Post* "fact"-checker asked, "Was the new coronavirus accidentally released from a Wuhan lab? It's doubtful," the "fact" check concluded.[18] And when Dr. Fauci dismissed the theory along with the rest of the press, CNN took the liberty to write, "Anthony Fauci just crushed Donald Trump's theory on the origins of the coronavirus."[19]

The narrative took hold so firmly that, upon taking office, President Joe Biden actually shut down a Trump-era State Department investigation into the origins of the virus.[20] But then, like the Russia bounty story, just over a year later, President Trump's assertion magically became credible in the eyes of the press. Doing a total and complete 180, Dr. Fauci said this when asked about the virus occurring naturally, "I am not convinced about that, I think we should continue to investigate what went on in China until we continue to find out to the best of our ability what happened."[21] Like a herd of blind sheep, the press fell in line. "Timeline: How the Wuhan lab-leak theory suddenly became credible," read a *Washington Post* headline.[22] The question, though, should not be why the lab-theory suddenly became credible, it should be why it was so easily dismissed. The answer to that is simple: so driven by animosity for President Trump, the press was willing to dispense with truth.

Lafayette Square

On the afternoon of Monday, June 1, 2020, President Trump walked to St. John's Church—the historic church that had been set on fire the previous night. When he arrived at the church, he held a Bible in the air. The secretary of defense, attorney general, national security advisor, chief of staff, and I all stood alongside the president as he sent a very clear signal that violence and lawlessness would not prevail. The press, for their part, decided they wanted to report a different version of events entirely.

"Peaceful Protesters Tear-Gassed To Clear Way For Trump Church Photo-Op," NPR declared.[23]

"Inside the push to tear-gas protesters ahead of a Trump photo op," the *Washington Post* wrote.[24]

"From Tiananmen Square to Lafayette Square," another absurd *Post* headline read.[25]

Joe Biden, Kamala Harris, Nancy Pelosi, and the Democrat party quickly seized on the narrative as the media continued to dig in. In a briefing two days later, CNN's Jim Acosta continued the falsehood. "Kayleigh, you mentioned Dr. King. He, likely, would not have approved of what took place Monday evening across from the White House, as you probably know. If the White House, the president, and his team had to do it all over again, would you have gassed and pummeled protesters to clear the park so the president could have a photo op?"[26]

I explained to the press corps that moving the protesters was not connected to President Trump's walk to the church. "[I]n the morning, AG Barr had determined that we needed to expand the perimeter by one block on each side," I told them. This would have been long before President Trump had decided to walk to the church. "He was surprised—AG Barr—when he arrived at the White House to see that that perimeter had not been moved," I continued. "So he said that we needed to get going with moving that perimeter. He told the officers that out there. That was late afternoon. So that decision was made in the morning...."[27] I also pointed out that "protesters were told three times over loudspeaker that they needed to move." Rather than clearing the area, the protesters began to throw bricks and frozen water bottles at officers.

But the truth was not acceptable to the press corps.

They continued with their false narrative until they were proven wrong a year later by the inspector general for the US Department of the Interior. "[W]e determined that the evidence did not support a finding that the USPP [the US Park Police] cleared the park on

June 1, 2020, so that then President Trump could enter the park," the IG report read.[28] Reflecting on the news, NBC wrote, "That finding, published Wednesday, is likely to surprise many critics of Trump, who have long asserted that the president or his attorney general ordered the operation to pave the way for an act of political theater."[29] Yes, the finding was sure to "surprise many critics"—critics and the media as well, but perhaps those are one and the same.

The Science

This disdain for all things Trump also led the press to discard "the science." While "experts" like Dr. Anthony Fauci may have oscillated from recommending no masks to wearing a mask to then wearing double masks, some of the science was always solid.[30] For instance, the science saying that children were able to go back to in-person learning. I pointed this out during a July press briefing. When asked about the president's stance on re-opening schools, I said, "[T]he president has said unmistakably that he wants schools to open, and I was just in the Oval talking to him about that…. [W]hen he says open, he means open in full—kids being able to attend each and every day at their school.[31]

"The science should not stand in the way of this. And as Dr. Scott Atlas said…'Of course, we can [do it]. Everyone else in the… Western world, our nations are doing it. We are the outlier here.'" I continued. "The science is very clear on this…. For instance, you look at the JAMA Pediatrics study of forty-six pediatric hospitals in North America that said the risk of critical illness from COVID is far less for children than that of seasonal flu."

I emphasized once more, "The science is on our side here, and we encourage for localities and states to just simply follow the science, open our schools. It's very damaging to our children: There is a lack of reporting of abuse; there's mental depressions that are not addressed;

suicidal ideations that are not addressed when students are not in school. Our schools are extremely important, they're essential, and they must reopen."

For anyone with half a brain or an ounce of integrity, what I was saying was crystal clear: the science is on our side. Open up!

For Jim Acosta, an out-of-context tweet was more appropriate. "The White House Press Secretary on Trump's push to reopen schools: 'The science should not stand in the way of this.'"[32] The tweet set off a firestorm. MSNBC ran chyrons that reflected Acosta's tweet. "The science should not stand in the way" was the line. "White House press secretary: 'The science should not stand in the way of' schools fully reopening," read the NBC headline.[33] Without context that I went on to say because "the science is on our side here," these liberal outlets were suggesting that I was instructing localities to *ignore* the science and reopen schools anyway. In fact, it was directly the opposite. I personally picked up the phone and called the bureau chief at NBC. Nevertheless, the inaccurate headlines persisted.

Even Jake Tapper, someone who is typically in line with his left-wing colleagues, stood up for me in the moment. "Folks read the ENTIRE McEnany comment about 'the science should not stand in the way' of opening schools. She's arguing that the science is on the side of those who want to open them, she cites a JAMA study. I'm not taking a position on the matter but be fair," he tweeted.[34]

Though I'm no fan of Tapper's "reporting"/editorializing, I did appreciate his exceedingly rare moment of truth. Acosta went on to add to his tweet: "McEnany went on to say 'the science is on our side here.'" In what is a shock to absolutely no one, his first, deceiving tweet got 47,000 retweets and a lot of fake news segments. His second follow-up? Well, that just got a paltry 797 retweets. The cleanup never makes up for the initial lie.

I spent many briefings thereafter talking about the importance of children being in schools. I cited the CDC director, who said that COVID-19 had "a very limited effect on kids.... Unlike the flu, kids are not driving the transmission cycle."[35] I urged reporters to look at the "holistic health" of the child, noting that one-fifth of all child abuse cases are reported by educational staff at a time when there was a decrease in child abuse cases being reported. I cited the American Academy of Pediatrics, which noted that "morbidity and mortality" among children would increase if schools stayed shuttered. I also pointed out that students of color were most impacted by this. "For students of color at all levels across the country, school closings create problems even more urgent than the interruption of their educations. Schools also serve as a community nexus for food and for housing," the NAACP pointed out.

But the facts were not of interest to the press; the politics were.

Hunter Biden

In October of 2020, the *New York Post* obtained emails from a laptop belonging to Hunter Biden, son of Democrat presidential nominee Joe Biden. The emails appeared to show Hunter "leveraging his connection to his father in a bid to boost his pay from a Ukrainian natural gas company," according to the *Post*.[36] The revelation should have been an explosive October surprise during a heated election year, prompting reporters to ask questions of Joe Biden and do some digging on the matter. That, of course, did not happen.

Instead of asking questions, the press went silent. "Obviously, we're not going with the *New York Post* story right now on Hunter Biden," CNN's political director said in leaked audio.[37] "We don't want to waste our time on stories that are not really stories, and we don't want to waste the listeners' and readers' time on stories that are just pure distractions," said an NPR managing editor.[38]

In addition to refusing to cover the story, the press went into "cover-up" mode. The emails had to be Russian disinformation! *Politico* confidently concluded, "Hunter Biden story is Russian disinfo, dozens of former intel officials say."[39] CNN also carried the narrative, reporting that "US authorities [are] investigating if recently published emails are tied to Russian disinformation effort targeting Biden."[40] The director of national intelligence, John Ratcliffe, rebutted the assertion, saying the emails were not Russian disinformation.[41] But the press didn't care.

Social media did its part in burying the story. Twitter removed the *New York Post* from its platform, demanding the *Post* delete the tweet, and Facebook stopped the report from being shared. The *New York Post* stood its ground amid the censorship, refusing to delete their tweets before ultimately being reinstated to their Twitter account.[42] I, too, was blocked from Twitter for sharing the story with my account only being reinstated after my daughter, Blake, deleted the story from my account. I couldn't bring myself to do it. "One day I will explain to her what censorship is and why she had to unjustly delete Mommy's tweet in order to speak!" I tweeted atop a photo of Blake pressing the delete button.[43]

Big Tech and Big Media had succeeded in delegitimizing the Hunter Biden story. That is, until after the election. In December of 2020, Hunter Biden himself revealed that he was under federal investigation. "I learned yesterday for the first time that the U.S. Attorney's Office in Delaware advised my legal counsel, also yesterday, that they are investigating my tax affairs," Hunter wrote.[44] A few months later, Hunter confessed that the laptop "certainly" "could be" his.[45] Of course the laptop containing thousands of pictures of Hunter, texts from Hunter, emails from Hunter was indeed Hunter's. But the press did not care, as they carried the water of the Democrat Party.

◦◦◦

THIS IS BUT A sampling of all that the press got wrong. They claimed we would not have a COVID-19 vaccine by the end of 2020. How dare President Trump suggest this?! He was right. They asserted that President Trump had instructed a Georgia election official to "find the fraud." They were wrong. When audio of the call leaked, the *Washington Post* was forced to correct their story. I could fill many more pages with examples like these, but I won't.[46]

The stories that the press failed to report accurately were stories of great consequence. If you had bought into the narratives set forth by the *New York Times*, CNN, and others, you believed that we had a commander in chief who refused to hold Russia accountable as they targeted US troops overseas. You believed we had a president callously calling our servicemen and women "losers" and "suckers." And you believed that we had a leader willing to tear gas protesters just to take a smiling photograph. All of these things were untrue, and yet all of them were reported to the American public. For all the media's talk about Russia influencing our election, perhaps it's time they look in the mirror.

CHAPTER 7

CRISIS COMMUNICATIONS

"Be of good cheer; I have overcome the world."

—*Excerpt from* JOHN 16:33

The sun was shining on that warm evening in Latrobe, Pennsylvania, as Air Force One touched down ahead of another Trump rally. The weather, unfortunately, would not be an omen for the news cycle on the horizon. A devastating story—perhaps the worst of President Trump's presidency—would interrupt the high energy event.

That evening, I descended the staircase of the presidential aircraft to throngs of excited rallygoers ready to see the president. "You've got to come see the overflow crowd," Chief of Staff Mark Meadows said to me shortly after the rally began. Sneaking behind the venue, Mark ushered me over to a crowd full of Trump supporters who could not enter the at-capacity tarmac rally but still wanted to show their support. Watching the president from a big screen, they were thrilled when Mark and I arrived at their overflow location. They might not be able to see the president live that night, but at least they could shake hands or take a picture with his chief of staff and his press secretary.

Mark and I interacted with the overflow crowd for about thirty minutes before heading back to the main event. This was just before everything went south. On the plane, my most trusted deputy press secretary, Judd Deere, had informed me about a story on the horizon. My memories on the matter are vague, but from what I recall, the inquiry told us that the story would involve the president and alleged remarks he had made via an anonymous source. The inquiry did not seem urgent, but indeed it was.

While I was standing on the tarmac, the *Atlantic* story published. "Trump: Americans Who Died in War Are 'Losers' and 'Suckers,'" read the headline. "The president has repeatedly disparaged the intelligence of service members, and asked that wounded veterans be kept out of military parades, multiple [ANONYMOUS] sources tell *The Atlantic*."

As the sun set that evening in Latrobe, several White House colleagues came up to me in panic mode.

"Kayleigh, what is this story?" one asked.

"Did you see this?" inquired another.

For the entire group of White House officials in Latrobe, the mood evolved from calm to chaos. Standing on the tarmac with a number of other senior aides, a frenzied rush of activity set in among the staff. In addition to alleging that President Trump had called our troops derogatory names, the story also claimed that the commander in chief had scrapped a visit to honor our troops at the Aisne-Marne American Cemetery in France, containing the graves of 2,300 fallen soldiers in World War I with the "Walls of the Missing" displaying 1,000 names of the missing.[1] The *Atlantic* story contended that President Trump had falsely blamed rain for the cancelation. "Why should I go to that cemetery? It's filled with losers," the story quotes the president as saying. Several of the senior aides I was surrounded by at that rally knew the story was false—because they were there.

Channeling my press shop's motto—"Offense Only"—I realized that we could fill an entire story with the firsthand accounts of people actually there with the president on the trip to France. They would happily go on the record and categorically deny the *Atlantic*'s premise. We just needed an honest reporter willing to write it.

In between the loud applauding and the repeated chanting of "four more years," I began to call former White House personnel who were in the room with the president during the events in question. One-by-one, I gathered their on-the-record quotes denying the *Atlantic*'s charges. Then, I called the reporter.

"Rob, can you hear me?" I asked. Rob Crilly of the *Washington Examiner* was a good reporter. I knew he would be interested in writing the White House's account of the story.

"I can barely hear you. I'm here at the rally and service is spotty," I remember him saying.

"I assume you've seen the *Atlantic* story," I said. "I have people willing to go on the record and challenge the reporting. Would you consider hearing them out?"

Rob was interested and said he would check with his editors amid the chaotic noise we were trying to work around.

The bright sunny day in Latrobe, Pennsylvania, was no longer with us. The sun had set, and the sky turned dark as President Trump ended his rally. "We will make America proud again. We will make America safe again. And we will make America great again!" the president concluded. President Trump started to walk down the catwalk as "Y.M.C.A." rang through the night sky. Joyous faces gazed at him, arms extended outward as he headed toward Air Force

One. I knew that at the end of that catwalk as he descended the stairs I would need to get his attention. It was imperative.

In the COVID-era, our rallies all took place on tarmacs. The president usually had a fairly short walk from AF1 to the stage and then back the same route upon conclusion. At the end of his rally, as he walked to the plane, a stream of aides would follow behind him. He would walk to the left, usually alone, and board a staircase made solely for the president. His aides would head right to an adjacent staircase and hurry on board, so as not to hold up takeoff. Behind us, the traveling members of the White House press corps would load.

During this walk, I would have to disrupt his smiles and waves and inform him about the story that just broke. It was essential because, occasionally—though not often after rallies—he would stop alongside the presidential aircraft and take a question or two from the press. If I didn't catch him before the walk, we ran the risk of President Trump taking questions, blissfully unaware of the slanderous story that had just popped.

After President Trump descended the staircase amid raucous cheers, one of his aides guided him in my direction. I paused for a moment, trying to find the words to deliver the news.

"Be quick," he said, completely aware that thousands of eyes were on us on the tarmac.

"Mr. President, a very bad story just popped in the *Atlantic*, saying that you disparaged our fallen soldiers. I don't want you to be blindsided by the press," I said before he walked away and headed to AF1.

Aboard Air Force One, I went to his private office space and reviewed the allegations with him point-by-point. He was deflated and completely bewildered at the accusation. While he was usually able to casually dismiss the stream of bad stories he endured during his presidency, this was not the case for the *Atlantic* story.

"What kind of monster would say this? I know monsters, and even they would not say it," I recall the commander in chief asking repeatedly over the days that followed. I can tell you, on a personal level, I have never seen the president so distraught over a report. I regularly came to him with bad news. For the most part, he seemed to take it with a grain of salt.

"Mr. President, we have another *New York Times* hit piece on your taxes," I would tell him once a week as we neared the election.

"You've gotta be kidding me," he would casually reply before changing the subject, totally unconcerned with the hit piece on the horizon. He was used to the negative press.

The *Atlantic* piece was different.

I spent the first part of my travel back to Washington, DC, working to get Rob all he would need for his report in the *Washington Examiner*. I supplied Rob with the accounts of several White House officials, corroborating that the trip to Aisne-Marne American Cemetery was scrapped due to weather, not the president's personal preference. I also passed along a November 10, 2018, email from the president's military aide detailing that a "Bad WX" or "bad weather call" had been determined, therefore sidelining the pre-planned trip.[2]

Several firsthand sources went on the record with Rob. "I was with the President in Paris, France when there was a bad weather call for the helo lift to the Aisne-Marne American Cemetery," Dan Scavino shared, noting that the *Atlantic* report was neither "accurate nor true."

Stephen Miller expounded, "The president deeply wanted to attend the memorial event in question and was deeply displeased by the bad weather call. The next day, he spoke at Suresnes American Cemetery in the pouring rain and refused an umbrella."

The *Atlantic* had outrageously reported that "Trump rejected the idea of the visit [to Aisne-Marne American Cemetery] because he feared his hair would become disheveled in the rain, and because he did not believe it important to honor American war dead...."[3] How could that possibly be true when, as Miller noted, the very next day, in pouring rain and while refusing an umbrella, President Trump honored American war heroes who had perished?

President Trump himself forcefully denied the *Atlantic* story that evening. With the White House traveling press pool huddled around him in the dark of night, he said to the reporters what he had expressed to me privately: "What animal would say such a thing? And especially since I've done more, I think more than almost anybody, to help our military to get the budgets, to get the pay raises for our military. So I just think it's a horrible thing that they are allowed to write that. We can refute it. We have other people that will refute it."

And refute it we did. The *Washington Examiner* piece I worked on was headlined: "White House officials deny Trump disparaged war dead and say he was 'livid' he could not visit French cemetery."[4] The next day, I held a White House press briefing, featuring Senior Advisor Jared Kushner and National Security Advisor Robert O'Brien. Jared denied that the president had ever spoken this way before going on to note an oddity in Washington. "Look, what I find in Washington [that] is strange, is sometimes you'll have a couple unnamed sources and the media treats that as a panacea. And then you'll have, you know, ten people on the record saying it didn't happen and you give no credence to that," Jared aptly observed.[5]

Standing at the podium, the national security advisor also issued a long and forceful denial, recalling all the times he had to make the difficult call to the president, sharing with him that a soldier had lost his life. "So I don't believe a word of what was in the *Atlantic* article," O'Brien said. "Because I've had two and a half years of working side

Landing in Goodyear, Arizona for a Trump rally just days before the 2020 presidential election.

Interacting with an energetic crowd at the Trump rally in Prescott, Arizona.

Aboard Air Force One after a Campaign rally, pregnant with my daughter, Baby Blake.

A Trump rallygoer prays over my nine-month pregnant belly in Tupelo, Mississippi.

Interviewing a Trump rallygoer in Albuquerque, New Mexico.

Baby Blake accompanies Mommy to the White House Christmas Party.

Baby Blake makes a visit to the Oval Office.

Walking Baby Blake along the West Colonnade to Halloween at the White House.

My husband and I walking along the West Colonnade after the Christmas-time congressional ball.

My parents, Baby Blake, and I walk along the West Colonnade.

President Trump and Florida Governor Ron DeSantis meet with White House staffers in the Oval Office.

Chief of Staff Mark Meadows whispering me a message in the Oval Office.

My first time taking questions from the podium in the James S. Brady Press Briefing Room on May 1, 2020.

Walking to the podium ahead of a White House press briefing as one of my top aides, Chad Gilmartin, takes his seat.

Taking questions from the White House press corps during one of my briefings.

COVID Taskforce Coordinator Dr. Deboarah Birx takes questions ahead of my White House press briefing.

President Trump and I walking along the West Colonnade to the Oval Office.

President Trump and I gaggling with reporters in the White House press corps before walking to Marine One.

President Trump and I walking back to the Oval Office after the President briefed reporters in the James S. Brady Press Briefing Room.

I watch as President Trump holds a briefing in the James S. Brady Press Briefing Room.

Tia Dufour (White House)

President Trump and I walk toward Marine One on the North Lawn.

Joyce Boghosian (White House)

President Trump and I stand in lower press and observe the network coverage on a cluster of television screens ahead of a White House press briefing.

Catching up with President Trump and Chief of Staff Mark Meadows ahead of a Make America Great Again rally in Washington, Michigan.

President Trump standing in front of St. John's Church, lit ablaze by rioters the previous night. After the president held up a Bible, Secretary of Defense Mark Esper, Attorney General Bill Barr, National Security Advisor Robert O'Brian, Chief of Staff Mark Meadows, and I join him in front of the desecrated Washington landmark.

Talking with President Trump ahead of an update on the border wall in Yuma, Arizona.

Attending church with President Trump, Hope Hicks, and Dan Scavino at the International Church of Las Vegas.

Shealah Craighead (White House)

Shealah Craighead (White House)

Arizona Governor Doug Ducey joins president in the Oval Office. Coronavirus Task Force Coordinator Dr. Deborah Birx and I sit on the couch as a group of reporters listen in.

On stage dancing to the YMCA with President Trump at the Villages in Florida.

Joining the president on stage at a rally in Prescott, Arizona.

President Trump and I speaking to a group of reporters before boarding Marine One for Joint Base Andrews.

Waiting to go on stage and speak at the Republican National Convention.

Speaking at the Republican National Convention about my BRCA2 genetic mutation and my decision to have a preventative double mastectomy.

My sister, Ryann McEnany, and I speak with President Trump ahead of a Make America Great Again rally in Henderson, Nevada.

Baby Blake stands behind the podium in the James S. Brady Press Briefing Room with Mommy.

by side with the president, and I've never seen anything like that. And I thought it was…pretty disappointing that some magazine would write that."

At the end of the briefing, I took to the lectern and expressed that the story had been "categorically debunked by eyewitnesses and contemporaneous documents." I put the email detailing the bad weather call on the screens behind me. I also brought the denials from two more on-the-record sources.

"I was with the President the morning after the scheduled visit. He was extremely disappointed that arrangements could not be made to get him to the site and that the trip had been canceled," Derek Lyons, staff secretary and counselor to the president, had written. "I have worked for the President for his entire administration…[and] I have never heard him utter a disparaging remark, of any kind, about our troops."

I then read to them another account from former Deputy Chief of Staff Dan Walsh: "I can attest to the fact that there was a bad weather call in France and that the helicopters were unable to safely make the flight. Overall, the president's support and respect for our American troops, past and present, is unquestionable."

That brought the number of on-the-record sources denying the story to ten—a number that would continue to grow. During a briefing a few days later, I highlighted for the press corps just how many people had refuted the story. "Now you have twenty-five people who have spoken out and dismissed this story," I said.[6] Even some of the president's critics had spoken out in his defense. Though President Trump and former Chief of Staff John Kelly did not end on the best of terms, Kelly's senior advisor, Zach Fuentes, went on the record and said, "You can put me on record denying that I spoke with the *Atlantic*. I don't know who the sources are. I did not hear POTUS call anyone losers.… Honestly, do you think General Kelly would have stood by and let ANYONE call fallen Marines losers?"[7] Former National Security Advisor John Bolton, who had written a book deriding Trump, also denied that he had heard him make these callous statements.[8]

I continued to make these points to reporters, but I also went on in that September briefing to note the *Atlantic* reporter's untrustworthy history: "Indeed, in the early 2000s, this author was then at the *New Yorker*, and he extensively wrote on the possible links between Iraq and al Qaeda, a suggested link that was key behind the decision of US involvement in Iraq. He relied on people who, in his words, quote, 'seem to me to be credible, who said that they had information about such connections between al Qaeda and Iraq.'"

"Yes, yes, I know I started the Iraq War," he later wrote in a sarcastic piece.[9]

"His reporting cannot be trusted," I said. "As noted by the fact that twenty-five people have come out on the record dismissing his report—the report by a liberal activist."

For anyone who knew the president, the allegations rang hollow. Even some reporters in the White House press corps noted this to me. President Trump had nothing but the utmost respect for our servicemen and women. This story was a shameless and baseless hit job against President Trump two months out from an election. Coincidentally (or not), bombshell stories became the norm in the lead-up to the 2020 election. The Russia bounty story, which had dropped in June of 2020, was less of a one-off and more of a trend. When you consider this slanderous *Atlantic* story, combined with the anonymously sourced and now discredited Russian bounties story, you are left to wonder whether this was a coordinated leak campaign against President Trump ahead of an election.

The anonymous source would plant the story with a left-wing publication. The press writ large would then run with it. And then the Democrat nominee would seize upon it. Just as he had seized on the Russia bounty story, then-Democrat presidential nominee, Joe Biden, of course took advantage of the *Atlantic* story, calling President Trump "unfit" to lead while saying, "I've never been as disappointed, in my whole career, with a leader that I've worked with.... If the article is true—and it appears to be, based on other things he's said—it's absolutely damning. It is a disgrace."[10] In the weeks before the election, the Biden campaign used the false reporting in ads, featuring a veteran expressing his dismay over the remarks.[11]

It was no secret that the military supported Trump, overwhelmingly. It was the job of the deep state to change that, and the press would willingly assist. They tried, but they failed. The effort to cleave away the president's military base did not succeed. As *Forbes* wrote just after the story published, "Military Households Still Back Trump Over Biden, Despite Bombshell Atlantic Report."[12]

I believe, though, that most of our military men and women saw right through the *Atlantic*'s reporting. Each day to and from the White House, a driver from the United States military would pick me up. Sometimes we would have conversations on the news of the day. On the night after one of my September briefings, a US Ranger picked me up. He told me how much he loved President Trump, and I felt compelled to tell him that the *Atlantic* story simply wasn't true. "President Trump loves our troops," I said to him. "That story is completely false."

"You don't have to tell me that ma'am," he said confidently. "I know it. He was our savior after Obama."

⌘

My time in the Trump White House was no doubt a crash course in crisis communications. Stories like the *Atlantic* "losers and suckers" story came regularly, and I had to exhibit calm amid fire. One such time came mere minutes before a press briefing when a bombshell story dropped. Literally minutes before a planned briefing on September 9, 2020, as we prepared to walk out to the James S. Brady Press Briefing Room, I looked up and saw a breaking news story on one of the televisions across from my desk.

"Woodward Book: Trump Knew In Early February Coronavirus Was Dangerous, Highly Contagious, Airborne, and 'Deadly,'" read the chyron, the text on the bottom of the screen on CNN. As I began to process the headline, graphics filled the screen—President Trump on the left and Bob Woodward on the right. An audio bar between them showed frequency waves going up and down, as if CNN had obtained some sort of audio.

"What in the world is this?" I thought.

I had heard about this Woodward book over the last few months, but I never—in my wildest dreams—anticipated an audio release of the president's conversations with the *Washington Post* journalist. I turned up the volume, and there were indeed audio recordings of the president's conversations.

I knew in that instant that virtually the entirety of my impending briefing would focus on these exchanges. A breaking news cycle minutes before taking the podium was less than ideal. As someone who prided myself on meticulous preparation, that would not be an option. A room full of reporters sat waiting for me. Canceling the briefing was not possible. We could delay the start of the briefing but not for long. Every moment past 12:00 p.m. that I wasn't at the podium was a moment for the press to speculate about the chaotic scrambling going on in the White House press secretary's office.

Scrambling was a bit of an understatement.

I wondered to myself whether CNN had planned the dropping of the tapes right around the White House briefing time. I do not know the answer to this. It certainly felt like it in the moment. What a coincidence (or not).

Though my heart had sunk for a moment at the realization that the entire focus of the briefing had changed, we did not panic. We immediately launched into new and additional preparation. There would not be time for in-depth research. There would not be time to create a binder of rebuttals. There would not even be time to make calls to officials across the administration to get an insight into the thought process of the administration at the time—a time when I was not even working in the building.

As press secretary, that is one of the biggest challenges. In addition to being in sync with your boss, the president, you have to thoroughly vet information. Various agency heads will come to you with information to use at the podium. Sometimes, that information will differ from what another agency head will tell you. Much of the time, you are asked about meetings or decision-making that you were not a part of. This means that you have to ask questions of the various agency heads across the federal government and vet the accuracy of what is presented to you to the best of your ability. In a crisis communications situation, which the Woodward tapes certainly was, the detailed, scrupulous process we would ordinarily put information through would not be an option. Fortunately, we had done so much research on COVID-19 previously and on the public comments of the administration, and some of this information would be useful.

As we continued to watch the breaking news on CNN, the leaders on the press staff had all huddled in my office, trying to ensure we had gathered every nuance of the breaking story as we came up with our responses. We began to piecemeal add pages to the binder. The binder—once perfectly tabbed—was now more of a hodgepodge of papers that I would have to be able to quickly reference.

The minutes ticked away in the 12:00 p.m. hour, and Julia began creating a timeline of administration actions and statements around the same time as the president's February and March conversations with Woodward. Part of the reason the Woodward calls from early February seemed so alarming on that September 9, 2020, day was because of the context of the moment. In February and March, we were just trying to understand the deadly coronavirus. Information was rapidly changing. The scale of what the pandemic would be was not yet fully grasped.

Indeed, when President Trump spoke to Woodward in February, just one American had died of COVID-19, reporting indicated.[13] When he spoke to him in March, there were just over 250 confirmed deaths.[14] While COVID-19 certainly had proven lethal, it was hard to imagine that more than half a million Americans would perish from this deadly illness. On that fall day in the White House, however, we knew exactly what we were facing—a global pandemic that had already ravaged the lives of so many worldwide.

Our preparation persisted that Wednesday afternoon. At this point we were far past our noon start time, and you could feel the intensity in the room. That's when Chief of Staff Mark Meadows walked into my office, now with about ten people seated around my desk. After talking briefly about the Woodward tapes, he said, "Let's pray."

As I mentioned previously, we prayed routinely before our briefings. Usually, the chief of staff's head of communications, Ben Williamson, would lead the prayer. Jokingly, I began to call him "Reverend Ben."

"Reverend Ben, it is time for the prayer," I would say before we all bowed our heads.

This time, though, it would be the chief of staff himself praying. He clearly recognized the anxiety of the moment and fittingly decided it would be him praying today. There's simply no doubt that Meadows was a great leader.

Taking a deep breath after the prayer, I reached for my *Jesus Calling* devotional on the far left edge of my desk. Sean had given me the small burgundy leather book when we were just dating. It had become a source of strength for me and also a way that I felt God communicated with me during times of adversity like this. I pulled the ribbon place marker from the bottom of the book, opening to the page I had left off on.

"Adversity" was today's topic.

Wow. How fitting.

"I have overcome the world; I have deprived it of power to harm you and have conquered it for you. In me, you are victorious," it read.

The accompanying verse displayed on the right-hand side of the page was John 16:33—"I have told you these things, so that in Me you may have [perfect] peace and confidence. In the world you will have tribulation and trials and distress and frustration; but be of good cheer [take courage; be confident, certain, undaunted]! For I have overcome the world. [I have deprived it of power to harm you and have conquered it for you.]"

This was the PERFECT verse. I believe God put it in my life, at that tumultuous moment. The verse prompted me to write this on the top of a page in my briefing binder: "In Me, you have [perfect] peace and confidence."

At 1:00 p.m.—a full hour beyond the briefing time—I descended the ramp toward lower press and said hello to the Secret Service agent stationed at the desk. I walked into the lower press offices and found my assistant press secretaries and press wranglers there waiting. I had three assistant press secretaries—Karoline Leavitt, Jalen Drummond, and Harrison Fields. They were like rays of sunshine each and every day—bright and enterprising, always with smiles on their faces. They are also fighters, completely loyal to the president and willing to battle in the trenches alongside him. Our press wranglers, Margo Martin, Gaby Hurt, and Davis Ingle were in charge of "wrangling" the press or corralling them out of the room at the conclusion of a presidential event. Margo, Gabby, and Davis are tough as nails, and the president always appreciated their ability to reign in an often unruly and loud group of reporters during key events. Margo, who had worked in the White House the longest, was a true leader on the press team and, like Judd, who had worked under prior press secretaries, was a blessing to have in the press shop. Judd, Karoline, Jalen, Harrison, Margo, Gaby, and Davis—an enviable team anyone would want at their side—were the group that waited for me in lower press ahead of each press briefing.

Before the Woodward briefing, I could tell they all recognized the weight of the moment. Standing in front of the blue door in my pink dress and hugging my briefing binder to my abdomen, I looked at Judd. "It's time." With the words "In Me, you have [perfect] peace and confidence" inscribed in handwriting on the top of my binder, I made it through that turbulent White House press briefing. The questions were tough, but with the help of my team, I was able to handle them despite having less prep time than usual. But, in the Woodward episode, I learned a life lesson.

The crisis communications mode in the White House gave me the opportunity to truly appreciate what it means to have peace in a time of adversity. No matter what challenge faced me, no matter how perilous the waters would get, there was always a Father prepared to walk beside me, if I would lean on Him. There would be a lot more leaning during my time in the Trump administration.

CHAPTER 8

The September Surprise

"Be alert and of sober mind. Your enemy the devil prowls around like a roaring lion looking for someone to devour."

—1 Peter 5:8

I t was late September, and America was still battling through the COVID-19 outbreak. We had endured a summer of violent protest, and a much-anticipated presidential election was about a month and a half away. At this point, it didn't seem like much could change ahead of that first Tuesday in November when Americans would cast their ballots.

Boy, was I wrong.

Not only would there be the dreaded "October surprise," there would be a September one too.

For the most part, I traveled with President Trump whenever he left Washington. If it was a weekday, I was always by his side. On weekends, I typically sent a deputy press secretary so that I could go home and visit my daughter and husband. As we headed toward the election, I made it a point to be present at every single trip with few exceptions. President Trump routinely sought my advice, and the stakes were too high to miss a day.

But on Friday, September 18, 2020, I grappled with sitting out the trip to Bemidji, Minnesota, for a campaign rally. It would be a quick trip—just one rally and then back to the White House. My mom, dad, Blake, and several aunts and uncles were in town. They wanted to see the White House, and I wanted to spend time with them.

Feeling a tinge of apprehension, I decided to let one of my deputy press secretaries, Brian Morgenstern, go on the trip in my place. Brian, an attorney and former assistant secretary at the Department of Treasury, was perfectly capable of handling the trip. But I made myself a compromise. I would turn down the trip, but I would agree to join Sean Hannity in the 9 p.m. hour from the White House lawn. This way, I could have an early evening dinner with my family followed by a late-night work obligation.

We started the evening at the Trump Hotel in Washington, DC, where we happened to run into Attorney General Bill Barr. He appeared to be with some of his team, and like me, he was unaware of just how consequential that evening would become. My family, all conservatives and big fans of Barr's tough, no-nonsense demeanor, were excited to see the attorney general and get their picture with him.

After meeting at the Trump Hotel, my family and I made our way to Filomena, a cozy, traditional-style Italian restaurant in George-town. When we descended the narrow stairwell into the dimly lit restaurant, the news cycle felt rather quiet, but I knew that could change at any moment. The president's rallies often made headlines, and he had just taken the stage in Minnesota. As I ate my penne alla vodka pasta, I kept my phone beside me so that I could monitor any developments. A few bites into my meal, my phone lit up with an incoming call. "Chad," it read. I knew I had to take it.

"Hey, what's up?" I asked.

In as frantic of a voice as I had ever heard from him, he said, "Ruth Bader Ginsburg just died!"

This couldn't be true.

"Are you sure?" I asked.

"Yes."

"*How is this possible?*" I thought. The rally I had chosen to sit out was the one where a legend on the Supreme Court had passed. President Trump needed me. This was a delicate communications situation, and he valued my opinion at times like these.

A burst of back-and-forth phone calls took place, as I called various colleagues on the ground in Minnesota. "We should honor her life in a statement," I said, not realizing the team on the ground already had a draft in the works. I spoke about the White House response with a variety of White House colleagues, as we mapped out the appropriate way to handle the news. One problem, though, the president was still on stage at the rally. The situation raised the question of when to tell the president what was obviously seismic political news that could impact his agenda and potentially the election. We had two options. Either we could pass the president a note on stage or wait to inform him after the rally concluded.

In December of 2019, while I was campaign press secretary, the White House team faced a similar decision as the House voted to impeach the president over an innocuous phone call. In that instant, the White House opted to interrupt his rally, sending me out to break the news to the president. Crouching in front of the adoring crowd, I moved within eyeshot of the president, holding a posterboard, reading "229-198"—the vote total for one of the two impeachment counts. "Oh, I think we have a vote coming in,"

President Trump said to the crowd in snowy Battle Creek, Michigan. "So, we got every single Republican voted for us. Whoa, whoa, wow, wow, almost 200! So, we had 198. 229-198. We didn't lose one Republican vote and three Democrats voted for us!" he concluded before thanking me.

Unlike with the impeachment news, in the case of the passing of Ruth Bader Ginsburg, we opted to wait to inform him. The impeachment vote was nothing more than a political stunt by Democrats—perfect for President Trump to discuss at his rally. As legal expert Jonathan Turley put it: the impeachment entailed "the shortest proceeding, with the thinnest evidentiary record, and the narrowest grounds ever used to impeach a president."[1] To put it simply, it was a sham! By contrast, what we were dealing with on the evening of September 18, 2020, was the death of an esteemed justice with the sacred constitutional responsibility to nominate a successor. The decision to wait in sharing this somber news with the president was the right one.

On stage, as his aides scrambled, President Trump said, "The next president will get one, two, three, or four Supreme Court justices. I had two. Many presidents have had none.... But the next one will have anywhere from one to four. Think of that. That will totally change when you talk about life, when you talk about [the] Second Amendment, when you talk about things that are so important to you. You're going to be stuck for forty years, thirty-five years, a long time. So this is going to be the most important election, in my opinion, in the history of our country. You got to get it right. Because if you don't get it right, we will not have a country anymore."

He had no idea how much meaning those words carried at this moment. President Trump was completely unaware that he would soon appoint his third Supreme Court justice of his presidency.

President Trump continued his nearly two-hour-long speech in Minnesota, and I rushed to conclude my Italian dinner and head back to the White House for my evening television hit with Sean Hannity. This appearance now held far more weight. I bolted across town with my family accompanying—some in the car with me and others in an overflow vehicle behind. We arrived at the White House, and I hurried them through security and into my office.

The political dynamic of the situation would eventually play out with the Trump administration rushing to fill RBG's vacancy ahead of the election, but tonight was a night for remembering the legacy of a dinosaur on the court. Though I vehemently disagreed with Justice Ginsburg's jurisprudence, I did respect her. Tonight, I would share that.

My family and I spent a short time in my office before walking out to Pebble Beach—the name for the area on the White House North Lawn where the press has its cameras stationed beneath a row of green tents. My family stood just off to the side of the Fox News tent as I quickly mic'ed up in preparation for my television appearance.

I knew this interview was important. With the president still on stage at his rally, I would be the first administration official reacting to the breaking news. I wanted to strike the right tone. I began by telling Sean Hannity that I had heard President Trump in private say how much he admired Ginsburg's tenacity.

"How can you not?" I asked. "She had a history of overcoming.... She lost her older sister, lost her mom before graduating high school. She went on to go to Harvard Law School...[where there were] nine women out of five hundred. Her husband got cancer in law school. She was raising a three-year-old daughter, taking care of her husband, on the law review, and worked to the top. She was a trailblazer for women…. Tonight, we honor her legacy. At the White House, we lowered the flag to half-staff."

Shortly after my Hannity hit, President Trump exited the rally stage in Minnesota to a crowd of cheering fans. This was the crucial moment. Elton John's "Tiny Dancer" echoed through the night sky as President Trump made his way toward Air Force One, the reporters in the traveling press pool huddled under the wing with much anticipation.

"The President May Have Been the Last Person in America to Find Out About RBG's Death," read one headline.[2]

Indeed.

President Trump reached the wing of Air Force One, and a reporter eagerly shouted the news. "Ruth Bader Ginsburg has died. Ruth Bader Ginsburg has passed away."

"She just died?" the president responded. "Wow, I didn't know that, you're telling me now for the first time. She led an amazing life, what else can you say? She was an amazing woman whether you agreed or not, she was an amazing woman who led an amazing life. I'm actually sad to hear that, I am sad to hear that."

Between my interview, the president's comments, and the White House's statement, we managed to keep the communication and the focus exactly where it should be that fall Friday evening—on honoring the life and legacy of Ruth Bader Ginsburg.

But the September surprise—the passing of a Supreme Court justice and subsequent nomination of another—some would speculate, prompted the October one.

⚭

JUST OVER A WEEK after RBG's passing, my mom, Blake, and I decided to go for a morning walk down the National Mall, leading up to the United States Capitol. It was a beautiful Saturday, and you could feel the cool, fall air that was on the horizon. We knew that the 2020 Prayer March was taking place, organized by Reverend Franklin Graham, and we wanted to check it out. We walked past the Smithsonian museums, wheeling Blake down the mall in her stroller. Christian preaching rang through the crowded sidewalks. Prayer filled the air. It was a beautiful sight and sound.

After we finished our walk, we rushed back to my apartment so that I could make it in time for President Trump's Fox News interview with Pete Hegseth. President Trump had agreed to interview with Fox just before the big event of that afternoon—the nomination of soon-to-be Justice Amy Coney Barrett. "ACB," as she would be dubbed, was a mother of seven. Known as a rigorous academic, one Notre Dame law school professor remarked, "Amy Coney is the best student I ever had."[3] Though it took President Trump over a week to nominate Barrett, I was fairly certain this would be his pick. In fact, the day after RBG's passing, President Trump and I had a phone call where he seemed somewhat resolute in nominating Barrett.

The Saturday afternoon of Barrett's nomination, I rushed up the stairs of the West Wing and into the West Wing lobby. I stopped when I saw several notable pastors congregated in a corner. I recognized many of the faces and stopped briefly to say hello. Among the group waiting to meet with President Trump was Reverend Franklin Graham. Reverend Graham's father was of course the late Reverend Billy Graham, affectionately known as "America's Pastor." Billy Graham had counseled every American president from President Truman on down. Now, here was Franklin Graham—a spiritual leader during the COVID-19 pandemic—at the White House to convene with President Trump.

Franklin, the president of Samaritan's Purse, a Christian humanitarian aid nonprofit, had rallied Christians into action amid the COVID-19 outbreak. When resources were sparse in New York City, Franklin's charity had set up a field hospital in Central Park. In addition to offering physical assistance, he also offered spiritual guidance to a grieving nation. On Easter Sunday, standing in front of the field hospital his organization had constructed, Franklin gave an Easter message called "America Together: Keeping the Faith." I watched his broadcast on Fox News from my Washington, DC, apartment. It was the first weekend after I had started my new job as press secretary.

Franklin began his sermon that Easter of 2020, talking about how we are "in the middle of a storm"—the storm of COVID-19. He ended his message by assuring the world that we don't need to be alone as we endure the storms of life. "That storm that you're going through. God doesn't give us a pass.... If you come to Christ, you don't get some kind of pass where you don't have to go through storms. No, you'll still have storms in life. You'll still have viruses or whatever else comes down our path in life. But He promises to be with us. He'll guide us. He'll direct us. He'll never leave us or forsake us if you put your faith in Jesus Christ."[4]

Franklin Graham was exactly right. Jesus Christ would guide us through the storm that was brewing right there in the White House.

In the West Wing lobby on that Saturday, I met Franklin for the first time. Inspired by all of his work and his testimony, I invited Reverend Graham to my office ahead of the president's Fox News interview and the subsequent nomination ceremony for Amy Coney Barrett. My assistant, Lyndee, also a woman of faith, wanted to meet Franklin. We took turns taking pictures with him in my office and sharing how much we admired his work. It was about an hour before President Trump would nominate Amy Coney Barrett to the Supreme Court in that infamous, alleged "superspreader" gathering.

Franklin left to meet with the president, and later that afternoon, I gathered in the Rose Garden, where President Trump officially announced his pick. "I stand before you today to fulfill one of my highest and most important duties under the United States Constitution: the nomination of a Supreme Court Justice.... Now we gather in the Rose Garden to continue our never-ending task of ensuring equal justice and preserving the impartial rule of law," President Trump began.

The ceremony, where I was seated just a few rows back from the podium, became the subject of much controversy. The history of the moment—the nomination of a Supreme Court justice just weeks before a presidential election—would be overshadowed by the events that followed. In the wake of the ceremony, an outbreak of COVID-19 plagued the White House. Dr. Fauci dubbed the gathering a "superspreader event."[5] The media, for its part, began displaying seating charts of the event, circling those affected one by one as new diagnoses seemed to emerge by the day.

Whether the event was the source of the coronavirus outbreak, we will never truly know.

In hindsight, I have thought a lot about that day. As a Christian, I believe that good and evil are constantly battling with one another here on earth. While God is ultimately in control and will prevail in the end, that doesn't stop evil from looming here on earth. 1 Peter 5:8 reads, "Be alert and of sober mind. Your enemy the devil prowls around like a roaring lion looking for someone to devour." I couldn't help but think that good versus evil dynamic was playing out in real time on that Saturday in September.

While Christ was at work on the National Mall during the 2020 Prayer March and in the West Wing as President Trump met with preachers, COVID-19 was lurking in our midst. A dim period was on our horizon.

CHAPTER 9

THE INVISIBLE ENEMY

"I've seen you move, You move the mountains.
And I believe, I'll see You do it again."

—ELEVATION WORSHIP

There's something interesting that I've discovered on the subject of evil, which as a world we experienced a lot of in the year 2020. Satan will find a way to rear his ugly head through a global pandemic, societal division, or death and destruction. But, make no mistake, Jesus Christ meets darkness with light. I saw it firsthand.

Thursday, October 1, 2020, was a day that I will never forget. On that Thursday, I held a White House press briefing. It was rather contentious—even more so than usual—but the events that followed would overshadow the back and forth of that afternoon's briefing. Following my briefing, I returned to my office to prepare to take off on Marine One with President Trump. The plan was to travel to Bedminster, New Jersey, for a political fundraiser. With no explanation, I was pulled down from the trip for no apparent reason.

"What is going on?" I wondered. *"I could use the break, but I hope everything is okay."*

But in a few short hours, I would soon find out why I was taken off the trip. Just after 8:00 p.m., Jennifer Jacobs from *Bloomberg* tweeted, "NEWS: Hope Hicks, who traveled with Trump aboard Air Force Once to and from the presidential debate on Tuesday, and to his Minnesota rally yesterday has coronavirus, sources tell me."

The tweet was accurate. I had been informed of the news a few hours before *Bloomberg* broke the news. The press immediately seized on the opportunity to begin criticizing the administration. "I'm told that a small group of officials were aware Thursday a.m. that Hope Hicks had tested positive. Despite that, President Trump traveled to New Jersey for a fundraiser and his press secretary held a briefing," Kaitlan Collins of CNN tweeted.[1]

I, for one, had no idea about Hope's diagnosis prior to my briefing. I held a briefing, entirely unaware of this fact. I was pulled off Marine One, entirely unaware of this fact. But I do not fault anyone in the administration for this. This was a rapidly moving situation, and contact tracing took time. Plus, while I had been around Hope both at the presidential debate and in Minnesota, there was a far bigger concern than informing the press secretary of Hope's COVID-positive status: Hope was around the leader of the free world. Should President Trump test positive, it would jeopardize the nation and potentially, in a worse case scenario, call into play the presidential line of succession. The enormity of the moment was not lost upon me.

I was in my DC apartment when the news of Hope's diagnosis broke to the public. My closest aide, Chad, had come over for dinner with my mom, Blake, and my sister, Ryann, who worked for the Trump campaign. As news broke, we quickly shifted from deciding what to order on Uber Eats to deliberating how to handle the breaking news. We eventually ordered Italian takeout food from Filomena. My Filomena outings and orderings seemed to forbode a critical moment on the horizon—either in the restaurant as RBG passed away or in my apartment as the biggest news story of my tenure was about to break.

Eating ravioli and meatballs, we tuned in to *Hannity*, knowing that President Trump had agreed to an interview on the program earlier in the day. As we anticipated, Sean Hannity asked about Hope's diagnosis. "She did test positive. She is a hard worker. A lot of masks. She wears masks a lot. She tested positive," the president replied. "I just went out for a test. It will come back later, I guess. And the First Lady also. We spend a lot of time with Hope and others. We will see what happens."

This did not strike me as out of the ordinary. At the White House, aides in close proximity to the president were tested daily for COVID-19. The president, now being a close contact of Hope's, was testing for the virus. At the moment, it did not set off alarm bells. But as the president was speaking on Fox News, I received a call from an aide in the chief of staff's office.

"The president and the First Lady have tested positive for COVID-19," they said.

"He tested positive on the rapid test and is awaiting his results on the PCR test to verify that it was not a false positive."

I was in total and complete disbelief.

"Was I learning this information before President Trump?" I wondered. I asked the chief of staff's aide whether the president knew about his positive test result, as he was talking live on national television. The aide did not know the answer to the question.

Chad, Ryann, my mom, and Blake had all heard the conversation. For a moment, we expressed our bewilderment, our fears, and the gravity of the situation. Then, Chad, Ryann, and I began to craft a tweet announcing the President of the United States' diagnosis of coronavirus. We knew, in the interest of keeping the public's trust, this diagnosis needed to be announced as expeditiously as possible. No matter how swiftly we drafted the tweet, however, we would need to wait for the positive diagnosis to be confirmed by the more accurate PCR test. This might take some time.

We drafted the tweet. We shared it with the team. And for TWO HOURS, we sat around, knowing the biggest story in the world was about to break. It was surreal.

During that time, I fielded a call from President Trump.

"What if I test positive?" I recall him repeatedly asking as we awaited his PCR result.

My sense was that he was asking me this question less out of worry for himself and more out of wanting to understand how the press would perceive and report a positive diagnosis. Like me, it was not lost upon him how pivotal this moment was from a communications perspective.

"You will rise above this, and America will rise with you," I told President Trump. "You are a victor."

"America is going to rally around you," I continued, before telling him that I was praying for him and the First Lady. "We will overcome."

As it turns out, the President of the United States did test positive that evening. Chad stayed at my house with my family until after midnight as we waited for the president to announce his result. Then, at 12:54 a.m., the news came out with President Trump tweeting out our draft tweet almost verbatim: "Tonight, @FLOTUS and I tested positive for COVID-19. We will begin our quarantine and recovery process immediately. We will get through this TOGETHER!"

Would we get through this?

I didn't know. I was genuinely scared. When I began my day, I never envisioned it would end like this. Who knew what tomorrow would hold?

The next morning I arrived at the White House to find it virtually empty. The chief of staff was there and some of his team. Jared was in as well. Outside of that, most offices were empty. The West Wing had an eerie feeling to it, especially without the president in the Oval Office.

"*Were we supposed to stay home?*" I wondered.

The press team, for the most part, showed up. We knew how high the stakes were. Of all my days in the White House, the communications and messaging were never so important as they were on October 2, 2020. The media had an array of questions. The world awaited updates on the president's status and prognosis. It was our job to deliver that.

A small group met in the chief of staff's office where we deliberated on whether he or I should go to "the sticks." The sticks were a collection of microphones positioned in front of a camera just outside the West Wing Lobby. If you wanted to drive a message or take questions in a way that was less formal than a press briefing, the sticks offered the opportunity to hold a casual question and answer session with reporters. The footage could then be used across all the networks. We decided this was the appropriate method of communicating an update on the president's diagnosis. We also determined that the gravity of the situation merited the chief of staff going to the sticks himself.

After our meeting, I returned to my office to brainstorm the questions Mark would be asked with my team. Mark and Jared soon walked in, and we briefed the chief of staff on what to expect at the sticks. As a press shop, our goal for this crucial day was twofold. First, we wanted to give accurate and regular updates to the American People on the president's condition. This meant providing tight and disciplined communication. Second, we wanted to instill a sense of calm across the country. While their president had been plagued by the invisible enemy, the business of the American People would carry on.

To that end, Mark would begin his gaggle touting the recent jobs report. The press, of course, only wanted to inquire about the COVID diagnosis, but we would start off with the jobs numbers, displaying calm amid crisis. We advised the chief to keep the gaggle short and to the point. This would be one update in a series of regular ones. During the back and forth, Mark shared that the president had "mild symptoms" but was "in good spirits" and "energetic," noting that the president had tasked him with five or six agenda items around 8:00 a.m. His first questions that morning were, "How's the economy doing?" and, "How are the stimulus talks going on Capitol Hill?" Mark revealed. Keeping the press interaction to right around seven minutes, Mark succeeded in providing the concise update we had hoped for.

It was my turn next.

A few hours later, I walked out to Pebble Beach to join Fox News, *Outnumbered Overtime* with Harris Faulkner and give the second update of the day on the president's status. Though I typically walked out confidently and set on the positive message I wanted to drive for the day, today was different. I wanted to continue the short, methodical answers based on the limited information I had on the president's health. Unlike any other day, when I would call up the president and ask him his thoughts on a topic, today I was relying on the secondhand information from the very small group around him.

The press was zealously in pursuit of information, and you could feel it. Reporters gathered around the sticks, hoping I would stop on the way back from my Fox interview to answer a few questions. Photographers huddled on the back side of the camera where I was doing my interview, snapping pictures of me as I took questions from Harris. During my interview, I echoed Mark's points about the president's "mild symptoms." I also brought new information that I had learned. The president had spoken with Majority Leader Mitch McConnell and Senator Lindsay Graham that morning. He had convened with Meadows to discuss emergency declarations for states, still at work for the American People. The interview went well, and I ended by calling out the *New York Times'* insane assertion that President Trump might not remain on the ballot in the wake of his COVID-19 diagnosis.

After the interview, I took a few questions at the sticks and then returned to my office to plan for the rest of the day. But the rest of the day would plan itself in a rather dramatic way. Unexpectedly, Tony Ornato, deputy chief of staff for White House operations, came into my office and asked to speak with me in private. We went into a side office, where he said that he needed to ask me a hypothetical question.

"Okay," I said, somewhat curious where he was heading with this.

"What if President Trump goes to Walter Reed?" he asked. "What is the press plan?"

"*Walter Reed? What?! How bad were the president's symptoms?*" I thought.

"Is this seriously a consideration?" I replied to Tony.

"I want to be ready for this circumstance," I remember him saying.

Walter Reed Medical Center offered world-renowned care. The military medical facility in Bethesda, Maryland, also had more capabilities than what could be provided from the White House. I was told that the move would be "precautionary," but that didn't ebb my concern. A somber mood set in as the staff slowly learned that this "hypothetical" would become a reality. My office sat right next to the Oval Office. Whatever was going on during my day, I knew—for the most part—that the president was just a short walk away. Today, there was a void, as he sat not in the Oval but in the White House residence. Now, he was leaving for Walter Reed. The idea of a White House without its commander in chief was a jarring thought.

To me, this was not just the president of the United States testing positive and being transported to a hospital. It was also a boss and a friend whom I grew to know and love battling this horrible, unknown illness. I had been with the president when he experienced tough times—whether it was losing a friend to COVID-19 (he lost several) or losing his own brother just a month and a half earlier.

I remember receiving a call from him on a Friday morning in August. "My brother's sick. He's not doing well. I'm going to go to New York to visit him in the hospital," he said. As I did during the hard times, I told the president I was praying for him. He was always grateful.

I knew how fond the president was of his brother, Robert. I hoped for the best but knew this would not be an easy few days.

Within an hour of that call, ABC had caught wind of the fact that Robert had been hospitalized. I told the reporter that the hospitalization was not due to COVID-19 and urged him not to report this information, as it was highly personal. But by 10:00 a.m. the story had popped: "Trump brother hospitalized in New York: Sources. President expected to visit brother, Robert Trump, sources said."[2]

President Trump made the trip to New York to visit his brother that afternoon, and I headed back to Florida to see my family. On that Saturday night, at around 10:00 p.m., I learned that the president's brother had passed. The media was starting to catch wind of it around the time that President Trump was being informed. I debated whether to call him so late in the evening on a Saturday, but

I decided it was too important. If Robert's death was reported in the news, I wanted it to be on the president's terms.

I called the White House switchboard, who reached out to the president.

"Kayleigh," the operator said. "The president."

Before he could speak, I expressed my condolences. "I am so sorry for your loss, but I can tell you with all the confidence in the world that I know you will see him again," I told the president. He thanked me for my kind words as he took in the news, surrounded by his family—the First Lady, Ivanka, Jared, and Eric were there from what I could gather. Together, we all began drafting a statement from the president announcing his brother's passing. Everyone chimed in with different ideas for the statement. I took notes on all of their thoughts from my home in Florida. I read several renditions of the statement, and I suggested to him that we add in the words, "We will meet again." He liked that.

After batting around a few versions of the statement, I hung up the phone to tidy it up. I called back a few minutes later to read the updated statement to the president and his family. The president continued to make edits until I read this final rendition: "It is with heavy heart I share that my wonderful brother, Robert, peacefully passed away tonight. He was not just my brother, he was my best friend. He will be greatly missed, but we will meet again. His memory will live on in my heart forever. Robert, I love you. Rest in peace."

It was a beautiful statement, and the president agreed. He wanted it to be perfect for his brother—all the way down to the two commas around "Robert." The president couldn't bring his brother back, but he wanted to do his memory justice. And he did.

We released the president's words in the form of a White House statement that evening. Before heading to sleep, I received one final call, this time from Jared. "Kayleigh, the president will be watching a virtual church service tomorrow morning. Can you call him and facilitate tweeting the link out so others can join in and watch?" I happily agreed before heading to sleep.

That's the kind of relationship I had with the president. He trusted me with the most sensitive of matters, like communicating the death of his beloved brother. The president and I spoke frequently, so I never had to ponder where he stood or what issues he was grappling with. But as he battled the invisible enemy, there was about a thirty-six-hour period where our communication was secondhand, usually through the chief of staff. The lack of direct communication just added to my mounting sense of worry.

As the press team sat in my office just before the president began his journey to Walter Reed, we were quieter than usual. Shaken and on-edge, we braced ourselves for what would come next. In order to get to Walter Reed, President Trump would have to walk from the Diplomatic Reception Room beneath the residence, across the South Lawn, and board the Marine One helicopter waiting to transport him. He would be passing a group of reporters along the way. Sitting in an empty White House, my press team decided that the president needed to see a show of support. We wanted him to look over and see his White House press team cheering him on, so we decided to file out to the South Lawn and watch his walk to the chopper.

Arriving on the South Lawn, we stood off to the side in an area usually reserved for a group of jubilant onlookers who had managed to secure a spot to watch a Marine One takeoff. Today, our White House press shop stood in their place. Instead of boarding Marine One with the president to head to a speech or a rally, I was an onlooker about to watch my boss from afar. None of us knew what to expect.

Before coming out to the lawn, I had sent out a memorandum from the president's physician. Dr. Sean Conley described the president as "fatigued" before going on to note that he had been treated with a "single 8 gram dose of Regeneron's polyclonal antibodies."[3] With little information, we wondered how the president would appear. Would he look frail or sickly? Those words seemed foreign to my boss, who always had more energy than his staff. It was hard to envision.

After waiting with great anticipation, President Trump finally emerged, walking out of the Diplomatic Reception Room and beneath the white awning overhead. Dressed in a navy suit, navy mask, and blue tie, he gave two quick thumbs up to the press before walking straight to Marine One, his thumbs up changing to a slight wave. Trailing behind him was Mark, about to board Marine One with a COVID-19 positive patient. As I saw the chief of staff in an N95 respirator walking behind the President of the United States, I thought to myself how unselfish and brave it was of Mark to accompany the president. My respect for Mark Meadows increased even more in that moment.

The president and the chief proceeded to the stairs of Marine One. The president did his customary salute to the marine standing to the left of the steps he was about to ascend, and on he went to the aircraft that would transport him to Walter Reed.

"This is surreal," Chad looked at me and remarked.

Surreal was an understatement.

THE NEXT DAY, I stayed in regular communication with those around President Trump at Walter Reed. From my DC apartment, in between changing diapers and watching cartoons with Blake, I tried to get regular updates on the president.

"He is holding court with the medical staff here," Dr. Conley said, a clear sign that the president's condition was improving. I smirked as he shared that with me. I knew exactly what he meant. President Trump always loved to banter in the Oval Office, questioning staffers and making observations. I was relieved to hear his lighthearted nature was back. The president and I quickly resumed our frequent conversations, and he also restarted his practice of dictating statements to me word for word. He was in great spirits. I had a feeling that we were out of the woods.

The rest of the White House, however, was not.

I showed up at work on Monday, prepared to join *Fox & Friends* from the White House lawn to kick off the week. In the White House, we continued to receive daily COVID-19 testing, and I made sure that I showed up early in the morning to be tested ahead of my hit. At this point, I had taken—in the very least—more than one hundred tests for the coronavirus. It was a daily routine. Unless you got a phone call, you knew that you were in the clear.

I took the test and ran back to my office to prep for the television appearance. I positioned my earpiece, phone, and notes in "go position" on my desk while I watched *Fox & Friends* on my big television. My phone rang, and I looked down to find a 202 area code number calling me.

"*Oh no,*" I immediately thought. "*Did I test positive for COVID-19?*"

"You've tested positive," the White House Medical Unit physician informed me.

Knowing that I was young with no preexisting conditions relevant to COVID-19, I knew that I would be fine. I didn't worry for my own health, but for my family. I wanted to make sure that my mom and young baby were protected in the small apartment we shared. I knew this meant I would have to be diligent about quarantining and staying away from everyone else.

I called to inform my family, and then my focus turned to canceling my television hit—now minutes away. I suspected that reporters would likely see that I had been promoted as coming up on *Fox & Friends* but then never actually made the appearance. That would certainly fuel speculation. Also, there was the possibility that someone in the White House leaked my diagnosis. I needed to get home, get quarantined, and release a statement about my diagnosis as quickly as possible.

I left White House grounds and set out for about a half-mile walk home. With a positive diagnosis, I obviously would not be getting in a car, potentially imperiling a driver. Unfortunately, I only had heels. I walked carefully along the sidewalk trying to take in the fresh air. I knew that I would soon be stuck in an apartment bedroom. Fresh air would not be readily available.

When I returned to my bedroom, I sat on my bed and began drafting a statement about my diagnosis. I knew, as with the president, it was important to be transparent. While the White House did not release a list of COVID-positive diagnoses, I thought it was important for a key public figure like me to be forthcoming, assuming I could get ahead of the rampant leaking. With that in mind, I quickly prepared a brief statement and released it on my Twitter feed, prompting a breaking news cycle.

"FOX NEWS ALERT! Half past the eleven o'clock hour on the east coast. We're getting the news right now—the White House Press Secretary Kayleigh McEnany has just confirmed that she has tested positive for the coronavirus," Sandra Smith reported. "She put out a statement. She says this: 'After testing negative consistently, including every day since Thursday, I tested positive for COVID-19 on Monday morning while experiencing no symptoms. No reporters, producers, or members of the press are listed as close contacts by the White House Medical Unit.... With my recent positive test, I will begin the quarantine process and will continue working on behalf of the American People remotely.'

"So the Press Secretary to the President is the latest to confirm she has tested positive for COVID-19," Sandra said. Indeed, my diagnosis came after many others. Beyond the president, the First Lady, and Hope, several others had tested positive—Counselor to the President Kellyanne Conway; the president's aide, Nick Luna; Campaign Manager Bill Stepien; RNC Chairman Ronna McDaniel; Senator Mike Lee; Senator Thom Tillis; Senator Ron Johnson; and Chris Christie. Other positive diagnoses were still on the horizon.

Sandra concluded her reporting on Fox News, saying, "And for so many of us who have known Kayleigh for so long, our thoughts and prayers for her and her family...[S]he has a young daughter at home. I don't even believe she's a year old yet. A baby."

She was right. I knew children generally were not affected by COVID-19 in the same way as adults, but of course, as a young mom, my daughter was of paramount concern. As I monitored the news coverage, my family prepared to leave and get a COVID-19 test themselves at a nearby medical facility. Over the next ten days, I took every precaution, making sure to stay quarantined. Fortunately, they all tested negative and were not affected by my diagnosis.

During quarantine, I did television interviews on my computer from the corner of my room and also answered reporter inquiries. The days got long in quarantine, but fortunately I discovered that my windows—while they did not open fully—cracked a good four inches. That was a relief! The bigger relief is that I never developed a single symptom from COVID-19. I was totally and completely asymptomatic.

As the days progressed, many other positive results followed. Thankfully, everyone in the White House made a full and complete recovery, including me. When I neared the end of my quarantine period, the White House required COVID patients to take a PCR test. Every day, I would walk outside—socially distanced—to the White House medical unit to take my PCR test. This test was the gold standard of testing. The PCR test ran cycles, described as being "like a washing machine."[4] Each cycle attempted to detect COVID's "genetic material," and upon detection it would cut off the cycles. If it cut off at or before thirty-five, the test was positive. The more cycles, the better.

On my first day, I tested at thirty-one. Such a disappointment. All I wanted to do was return to work. The president had fully recovered, and I was ready to go.

On my second day, my number went to 33.5. Frustrated at the slight progress, I did endless research about how quickly my number could go up. Even though I likely could not transmit virus at this point, the medical unit operated, rightfully, out of an abundance of caution. I knew the president had a multi-state trip full of rallies ahead, and I wanted to join. From Michigan to Wisconsin to Nevada to California to Arizona, he had a jam-packed schedule, and I was ready to get back out on the road. I had one more chance at this PCR test.

On that third day, I walked to my test. It was sunny and warm, and I was feeling optimistic. I took my test and walked back to my apartment, awaiting my results. I got a call from the medical unit.

"You got a forty-one!"

I was totally in the clear. A burst of joy filled me as I picked up my eleven-month-old daughter and gave her a big kiss on the cheek. We took a selfie together. It had been far too long! I was finally cleared to get back on the campaign trail, and I was ready.

ON THAT FIRST TRIP back with the president after COVID-19, we had a number of rallies on the schedule—on Saturday, Sunday, and beyond. Weekend rallies were typical during campaign season. But we had another stop on the campaign trail a little more out of the ordinary that Sunday: church. While going to church has been and continues to be part of my life, attending church on the campaign trail was a near impossibility when traveling with the president. The motorcade left early, and the journeys often ended late in the evening. This Sunday, however, President Trump was carving out time for church at the International Church of Las Vegas. I attended church regularly with my family but never with the President.

"*This should be an experience*," I thought.

When we arrived at the church, we entered through the side door. The congregation had already started their fellowship, and the president along with his team was placed in a holding room. Before an usher hurried me out to my seat in the front row, I snapped a picture of the beautiful donuts the church had laid out (never a bad thing to discover on a Sunday!). I arrived at a row of five empty green chairs, and I took a seat at the end, reserving the others for Dan, Hope, and the president.

I stood before a stage of men and women, singing beautiful lyrics in front of an American flag and beneath a room full of multicolored flags from countries around the world. As a Christian, I had heard many of the lyrics they sang previously, but for some reason, they touched my heart as if I were hearing them for the first time. I had sung the lyrics of "Do It Again" growing up in my hometown church, but here they were in a new context, assuring us all that Christ would find a way when we faced an insurmountable circumstance, moving mountains in the process.[5] Nothing could stand in the way of God's power.

The familiar lyrics I heard could not be truer. Many times in my life, I felt there was no way. Be it going through a crushing breakup, reaching a blockade in my career, dealing with the diagnosis of a breast cancer gene, there were storms in life. But when I saw a wall, God saw a way, ending in a beautiful marriage, a promising career, and a clean bill of health. He always made a way.

As I reflected on the beautiful words and waited for the president to enter the room, a new song rang out—one that I had never heard. In "New Wine" by Hillsong, the vocalist sang about the process of creating wine. The crushing and the pressing of the grapes created "new wine," just as God would use the figurative crushing and pressing of life's most challenging circumstances to bring about something new and beautiful if you let him.[6] The powerful lyrics were about yielding to Christ and trusting Him during the hard times.

"*Wow,*" I thought as I reflected on these words. "*How powerful.*" The trials in my life had been minor compared to many others who had experienced tragic and inconsolable loss. Before going into politics, I had interviewed so many moms and dads who lost children to terrorism, to gun violence, to a drunk driver.[7] Despite their tragedy, I was inspired by their faith, by their hope. Despite their sorrow, I recognized a joy rooted in Christ. These lyrics said it all.

As I listened to the song, a tear started to roll down my cheek.

You could feel the Holy Spirit in the room.

You could feel hope—hope despite a COVID-19 pandemic still grasping a broken nation.

Despite the death, the loss, and the pain, the invisible enemy had an unstoppable foe. His name was Jesus Christ.

CHAPTER 10

THE DEBATES

"For where two or three gather in My name,
there am I with them."

—MATTHEW 18:20

The clock was nearing 9:00 p.m., and you could cut the tension with a knife. Mark Meadows, Jared Kushner, Dan Scavino, Stephen Miller, Derek Lyons, and I walked down the hall of the JW Marriott in Nashville, Tennessee, toward President Trump's hotel room. Arguably, the single biggest moment of the presidential election was moments away: the final presidential debate. A lot was on the line. It would be President Trump's last opportunity to communicate with the American People in the venue that offered him the greatest reach.

The second presidential debate had been canceled, due to the president's COVID-19 diagnosis. This was a sham excuse. The debate was scheduled for a full two weeks after the president's diagnosis. According to CDC guidelines, "You can be around others after: 10 days since symptoms first appeared and 24 hours with no fever without the use of fever-reducing medications and other symptoms of COVID-19 are improving" [emphasis in original].[1] All of these things were true of President Trump. On top of that, he would have a PCR test to confirm he was not a transmission risk. But the notoriously liberal Commission on Presidential Debates canceled the second debate anyway. So much for following the science.

In practice, this meant President Trump lost a valuable opportunity to speak to the American People and to put Joe Biden in a format in which he simply did not thrive. With the loss of the second presidential debate, we knew that the stakes were that much higher for the third and final presidential debate. Compounding the pressure was the outcome of the first debate. I personally liked President Trump's first debate and his ability to go on offense, but the media spun the debate as chaotic and out of control. Some allies dubbed the debate a "missed opportunity."[2]

Among those "allies" was the very person who led the president's debate preparation—Chris Christie. Christie, alongside a small group of senior aides and Rudy Giuliani, prepped the president in a series of debate prep sessions, leading up to the September 29th debate. I was not involved in the debate preparation, so I cannot speak to precisely what happened during those sessions. In the aftermath of the debate, Christie summed up the president's performance this way: "[I]t was too hot. You come in and decide you want to be aggressive, and I think it was the right thing to be aggressive... but that was too hot."[3]

The president, for his part, had expressed to me that he was not taking this first presidential debate lightly. Despite Biden's constant gaffe-ridden and sometimes nonsensical speech, President Trump did not underestimate or marginalize the debate ahead. He told me that the former Vice President had a forty-year political career, which involved debating. While the expectations were low for Biden, he believed that Biden could be sharper than the very low expectation that had been set for him. Even a mediocre performance would be portrayed by the press as outstanding. I think this influenced his strategy of constant and protracted offense.

Despite not being in those first debate sessions, I did have constant access to the president. And while I did not go over the myriad of topics to come, I did have one point that I was determined would make its way into that first debate. I had a feeling that amid a healthcare discussion, President Biden would tie healthcare to the nearly two hundred thousand Americans who had died of COVID-19. In response, I wanted President Trump to bring up the extraordinary and unacceptable number of veterans who had died in the Obama-Biden VA healthcare system. The number was striking: 307,000 according to a VA inspector general report as noted in a CNN article.[4] In the event that Biden did what I anticipated, President Trump needed to know this fact.

As the president's press secretary, I knew how to prep him. In my view, it wasn't through the formal sitdowns at a long table in the elaborate Diplomatic Room. No, it was through constantly delivering the president your advice in an informal setting or in a private, casual back and forth. This is exactly what I did. I continually displayed for him a copy of the CNN article, headlined: "307,000 veterans may have died awaiting Veteran Affairs health care, report says."[5]

"Have you seen this?" I asked in the Oval Office.

"Have you seen this?" I repeated on Air Force One.

I went to his assistant and slipped the article into his private stash of documents for review ahead of the debate. I even handed it to him personally.

"I know," he said with exasperation.

It wasn't that President Trump needed a constant reminder. Not at all. In fact, President Trump had a great memory, often recalling moments or exchanges that I had forgotten. But I knew that he was the leader of the free world and had quite a bit going on ahead of the debate. A constant reminder never hurt. In total, I had probably put that article in front of him ten times.

And it worked.

Literally, mere minutes into that first debate, President Biden said, "Two hundred thousand people have died on his watch.... Seven million people have contracted COVID. What does it mean for them going forward if you strike down the Affordable Care Act?"[6]

With perfect precision, President Trump replied, "Joe, you've had 308,000 military people dying because you couldn't provide them proper health care in the military. So, don't tell me about this."

Predictably, Biden didn't answer the charge—because he could not.

In the wake of this "chaotic" debate, as the media described it, I knew I wanted to help with the final one. I was permitted to do this, so long as it was in my personal capacity, and I resolved to do just that. I knew that, in his gut, the president had the right answers. He didn't need to be briefed on his successes. He didn't need to be reminded of his accomplishments. He had that. Where I could help was in providing creative "pivot points" on the hardest topics that would emerge.

How could we make the most hostile topics in the debate our strength?

With that in mind, I developed a one-pager of "Debate Game Changers." These were moments that could turn the tide of a debate. My vision for this page was to offer the president statements or questions that could change the mind of a voter. In addition to this one-pager, I developed six more pages. Each page was titled with one of the six topics that the debate moderator, NBC's Kristen

Welker, had listed: fighting COVID, American families, race in America, climate change, national security, and leadership.

The pages were not intended to describe in great detail the numbers and statistics that would footnote the president's broader point. He already had that in his mind. Rather, the pages were meant to equip him with "Offense Only" points that he could use to change the defensive posture of the situation, much like what I did in my briefings.

On pandemic response, in addition to reminding the country of Operation Warp Speed (which we anticipated would deliver a vaccine in record time) and the work to secure large amounts of medical supplies and ventilators, it was important to point out that Joe had a record on pandemic response as well: his response to the H1N1 pandemic during the Obama administration. Biden's own chief of staff, Ron Klain, had admitted in 2019, "Sixty million Americans got H1N1 in that period of time and it's just purely fortuity that this isn't one of the great mass casualty events in American history. It had nothing to do with us doing anything right, it just had to do with luck."[7] What an admission! The American People needed to be reminded of this.

On national security, voters needed to know what the media refused to report: Joe Biden's family took $3.5 million from Russia; took millions from China with a 10 percent cut for "the Big Guy" (presumed to be Biden); and Hunter, of course, took millions from a corrupt Ukrainian firm with Joe himself bragging about firing the prosecutor prodding the company.[8] On climate change, my top-line point for the president was this: "Joe Biden cares more about appeasing radical left environmentalists than protecting the jobs of American workers," noting that Joe had said he will ban fracking and that he had endorsed the Green New Deal. In other words, AOC was totally in control.

And, on the economy, I wanted voters to understand that a Joe Biden presidency would cost American families $6,500 in median household income.[9] Under President Trump, real median income rose by "nearly 50% more than during the eight years" of Obama/ Biden, with "lower and middle-class Americans enjoy[ing] the largest gains relative to the Obama presidency."[10] Moreover, as the *Wall Street Journal* pointed out, "median household incomes increased more among Hispanics (7.1%), blacks (7.9%), Asians (10.6%) and foreign-born workers (8.5%) versus whites (5.7%) and native-born Americans (6.2%)."[11] President Trump had created a more inclusive economy, and the numbers told the story.

Using information like this, I worked to offer President Trump smart pivots and real moments that would land with viewers. Jared Kushner, Stephen Miller, and Jason Miller all reviewed and liked these points for the third debate. It was a team effort, and a much different preparation strategy than the first go-around. I walked through some of my points with him privately in three short, sporadic sessions. As with my point for the first debate on the loss of 307,000 veterans, I continually provided the president with my seven-page debate prep document. On debate day, I kept reminding him of the key points and called him twice as the debate approached, offering new information that dawned on me.

During one call, I said, "Mr. President, I just wanted to point out that Obama/Biden had a 'pandemic playbook.'" I had personally reviewed this "plan," which made continual reference to working with the China-centric World Health Organization (WHO). This is the same WHO that misled us on COVID-19's ability to transmit human to human, as they carried China's deceptive talking point. The playbook also mentioned relying on the virus' "host country"— as if working with China would work, the same country that barred

United States scientists from entering the country and had failed to block travel out of Wuhan at the outset of the pandemic.[12]

"Biden's playbook is China's playbook," I told the president.

I called President Trump a second time, with another thought—this one presented to me by a few of my colleagues. I passed along the message. "Mr. President, you should challenge the former vice president to say, 'Hire American.' It would go something like this: 'Joe, you like to plagiarize half of my plan—Buy American. But I never hear you say the second half—'Hire American.' I bet you won't say the words 'Hire American.'" The words, seemingly uncontroversial as they may be, would have angered Biden's radical left base who perceived "Hire American" as xenophobic. In the alternative, if Biden had refused to say, "Hire American," it would have been an enormous blunder as American workers suffered job loss amid the COVID-19 pandemic. It was a lose-lose situation for the then-Democrat nominee for president.

After my two calls, I went back to sit in a common area with my fellow senior staffers. We were all camped out in the executive lounge of the hotel, watching the minutes tick down to the time we would depart for the debate. Shortly before our departure, Mark came in and summoned me, Dan, Jared, Stephen, and Derek to follow him to President Trump's room. As a group, we would ask him a few mock questions, reviewing some of the tougher topics that were destined to come up. When we arrived, the president was in good spirits.

I cautiously tossed a few questions his way. So did others in our group, as we convened in a circle in the living room area of the suite. As we prepped, the president's family came in—Ivanka, Lara, Eric, and Don, as I recall. They said goodbye, knowing the next time they would see him, he would be on the debate stage across from Joe Biden. Our group continued our preparation, asking the president mock questions and discussing his answers. President Trump's answers during our prep session that evening were fact-driven, smart, and delivered in the perfect tone. I knew he was ready.

We left his room and loaded into the presidential motorcade, prepared for the five-minute motorcade ride to the Curb Event Center at Belmont University in Nashville, where the debate would be held. As with my briefings, more important than the actual preparation was the spiritual outreach. That morning, before I left for Tennessee, a group of aides and I gathered, and we prayed. I streamed a church service in the background—the same service that had been so meaningful at the International Church of Las Vegas that I had attended with the president.

Those beautiful lyrics rang out again, assuring us all that God had the power to move mountains.[13]

As the song filled my office, we bowed our heads, each person offering a prayer out loud detailing what was on their heart. It is my belief that the serenity I saw in the president ahead of that debate came from Christ. Many men and women across the country were praying. It made a difference. After all, Matthew 18:20 says this: "For where two or three gather in my name, there am I with them."[14]

When we arrived at the Curb Event Center that consequential evening, a few of us gathered in a small room with the president. The room was quiet. The president was calmly taking in the moment. President Trump looked in the mirror, preparing to head to the debate stage, as he straightened his red tie and watched Fox News' pre-debate coverage. The blue-lit stage awaited him. Two empty podiums sat beneath a red, white, and blue strip of stars. Above the two podiums was an eagle, perched upon an American flag, wings extended with a white ribbon surrounding our nation's emblem. The ribbon displayed the words "the union and the Constitution forever."

We had arrived at this debate set earlier in the day before heading to the JW Marriott. Both candidates had an opportunity to survey the lighting and the set. When we arrived, there were two huge and obtrusive sheets of plexiglass on the side of each podium. President Trump absolutely hated the glass barriers.

"I can see my reflection, and I will hardly be able to see Joe," he said. "I want to be able to look him in the eye."

Standing off to the side, I watched as Mark, the president's dutiful chief of staff, told the Commission on Presidential Debates that the barriers needed to be removed. The head of the commission claimed that the plexiglass was a "coronavirus precaution." The assertion was absolutely ludicrous. Both candidates had been tested. President Trump was fully recovered from COVID-19. The candidates were more than six-feet socially distanced—by a longshot. There was no scientific reason for the barriers. We all knew it. As the rest of the staff and the president loaded back into the presidential motorcade, Mark stayed behind to advocate for the plexiglass removal. I was told by a colleague that he had even gotten the liberals' COVID-go-to Dr. Anthony Fauci on the phone to advise on the matter.

Thanks to Mark's diligent work, he got his way. "Thursday night's presidential debate will not feature plexiglass partitions after all," the *New York Post* read. "Fauci 'agreed that the plexiglass wouldn't do anything,'" the president of the commission noted.[15]

Just before 9:00 p.m. that evening, we gave the president our last encouraging words, and he went to stand just off stage for his walk out. An aide told me that there was a free seat in the audience if I preferred to watch from where the president's friends and family sat. As great as that sounded, I decided to stay backstage. I wanted to work and take diligent notes on every moment.

Shortly after the clock struck nine, President Trump and the Democrat presidential nominee, Joe Biden, walked onto the plexiglass-free stage to applause. The first question was on COVID-19, and it went to President Trump. His answer, filled with statistics and facts, walked the viewers through his procurement of therapeutics, ventilators, and (soon) a vaccine. As the discussion proceeded, he hit the very point I hoped he would: "And frankly, he [Biden] ran the H1N1 swine flu and it was a total disaster. Far less lethal, but it was a total disaster. Had that had this kind of numbers, seven hundred thousand people would be dead right now, but it was a far less lethal disease. Look, his own person who ran that for him, who, as you know, was his chief of staff said, 'It was catastrophic. It was horrible. We didn't know what we were doing.' Now he comes up and he tells us how to do this."

Offense Only—but this time on a presidential debate stage.

Later in the debate, when Biden launched into an old, tired, and provenly false allegation that Trump was somehow a Russian pawn, President Trump was ready. "He's being fed information that is Russian, that is not true." Biden claimed. "And then what happens? Nothing happens.... Russia is wanting to make sure that I do not get elected the next president of the United States because they know I know them, and they know me. I don't understand why this president is unwilling to take on Putin when he's actually paying bounties to kill American soldiers in Afghanistan, when he's engaged in activities that are trying to destabilize all of NATO. I don't know why he doesn't do it but it's worth asking the question. Why isn't that being done?"[16]

So shameful.

As I mentioned earlier in this book, we now know that even the Biden administration has debunked the Russian bounty story.[17] But the truth didn't stop Biden from using this lie on a presidential debate stage.

And as it pertains to Afghanistan, the facts on the ground also did not stop now-President Biden from recklessly withdrawing our troops, causing the entire country to fall to the Taliban and leaving thousands of Americans behind. As I write this at the end of August, in the span of a few days, President Biden managed to undo the good work that our servicemen and women had done over the span of twenty years. Underscoring just how big of a cataclysmic failure the Biden withdrawal actually was, President Biden had to deploy more troops than he withdrew in order to fix his self-inflicted mess. Tragically, several American troops lost their lives in the process.

We also know that Joe had no desire to stand up to Putin as he tried "to destabilize all of NATO." No, in fact, we now know that Joe would greenlight the Nord Stream 2 pipeline between Germany and Russia—a project his own press secretary described as a "Russian geopolitical project that threatens European energy security."[18] David Harsanyi of the *New York Post* posed this question on the matter: "What does Vladimir Putin have on Joe Biden?"[19]

President Trump knew, and he revealed it in that very moment in the final presidential debate: "Joe got three and a half million dollars from Russia. And it came through Putin, because he was very friendly with the former mayor of Moscow and it was the mayor of Moscow's wife.... Your family got three and a half million dollars.... I never got any money from Russia. I don't get money from Russia.... [T] here has been nobody tougher to Russia...., Between the sanctions between all of what I've done with NATO. You know, I've got the NATO countries to put up an extra one hundred and thirty billion dollars, going to four hundred and twenty billion dollars a year, that's to guard against Russia.... I sold tank busters to Ukraine."

President Trump went on to hold Biden accountable on China and Ukraine, reiterating the points I had listed out for him: "Number two, I don't make money from China, you do. I don't make money from Ukraine, you do. I don't make money from Russia. You made three and a half million dollars, Joe, and your son gave you. They even have a statement that we have to give ten percent to the big man. You're the big man."

This was key, and likely the first time many Americans had heard about Joe Biden's nebulous ties to our adversaries via his son, Hunter. President Trump, in this moment, shared with sixty-three million voters a storyline they had likely never heard. After all, Twitter banned the *New York Post* (and me) for sharing the story on their platform. No one, other than Fox News and the *New York Post*, covered the story. Outside of certain segments of the population, many had never heard this information. In a maddening reversal, Twitter's CEO now claims it was a "total mistake" for blocking this information from the American public.[20] At the time, they barred me and others from the platform until we deleted the explosive story.

It was censorship. And it was also Big Tech, Big Media election interference. We now know that "one in six Biden voters would have changed their vote if they had known about scandals suppressed by media," including the Hunter Biden story.[21] While the president reached sixty-three million voters from that debate stage on this topic, it couldn't overcome the continual silence on the matter from major media platforms.

Near the end of the debate, President Trump hit another key point I hoped he would, and he did it perfectly. When climate change came up, President Trump hit the exact fact: Experts "came out and said very strong, 'Six thousand five hundred dollars will be taken away from families under his [Biden's] plan,' that his plan is an economic disaster. If you look at what he wants to do, you know the, if you look at his plan, his environmental plan, you know who developed it? AOC plus three." And then rounding out the debate, President Trump drove home the inclusive economy he had created, noting the significant gains in unemployment numbers and income for Hispanic, Black, and Asian Americans.

"Success is going to bring us together," President Trump noted in his final answer of the debate.

It was a great message, and for President Trump, a triumphant final debate.

"You killed it," I told him. "So, so good."

When he emerged from the debate stage, he was jubilant. He knew how well he had done. Before departing the venue, he went to a room where his campaign staff sat working. He thanked everyone for their work before getting into the presidential limo—the Beast— and heading for Air Force One. As the reviews came in, it was clear that President Trump had won the debate.

Even the critics noted Trump's success, albeit in a somewhat disappointed tone.

"[I]t's fair to say President Trump got in a couple of clean hits when it came to Vice President Biden," CNN's Jake Tapper acknowledged.[22] Adding that "Biden struggled when Trump confronted him with the question of, 'You've been in politics for forty-seven years. You were vice president for eight years. Why didn't you do that then?'"[23]

"He [Trump] actually had a theme at times," ABC's Jon Karl noted. "The theme that Joe Biden is a politician. When Biden would come up with something, 'Why didn't you do it in when you were in power? Forty-seven years. Why didn't you do it?"[24]

Paula Reid of CBS said, "The other part of the strategy was to bring up Biden's son, Hunter. Put those accusations into the mainstream and put them in front of tens of millions of voters. It appears on those two points, he succeeded."[25]

Indeed, that was a big a part of the strategy. I had mentioned, on several occasions, to the president that he should pivot to Hunter Biden. On climate change, I told him—after mentioning his record on the environment—he should pose the question: "Joe, how can you say you're good on climate change when you're on China's payroll?" China, of course, was the chief emitter of CO2. "Hunter Biden and the 'Big Guy' SOLD OUT to China, receiving millions while on the taxpayers' dime," I suggested he emphasize.

I remember being on Marine One with him, sitting on the seat adjacent to the commander in chief's prominent chair and running through potential debate scenarios like this. Even then, he nailed it.

While undoubtedly there were many players who contributed to the president's success that late October night during the final presidential debate, I think I played a part. I remember, sometime on debate day, Derek Lyons said to me, "You were the perfect person at the perfect time for this."

At this point, I had worked for the president for six months. I knew how he prepped, and I used that knowledge to help as best I could. Every president consumes facts differently. Some liked verbal briefings. Others liked a big stack of written documents. It was all personal preference. During my time in the White House, I had learned about the way President Trump consumed information. Formal, scripted remarks were always met with a presidential sharpie, doing real-time edits ahead of a briefing. For question and answer periods, it was best to isolate the most important question or two and provide the president with the top-line point he would want to pull out and share with the press corps.

I think the key defining characteristic of my preparation for the final debate was creating that seven-page document with key pivot points that he could deploy. It was tailored to his style and method of consumption. As a trusted colleague of mine said, "It was a resource to him that we built, based on his preference." I believe that our preparation left Biden on his heels.

But as with the preparation for my briefings, no amount of preparation would overcome the power of "where two or more gather in My name."

CHAPTER 11

THE CAMPAIGN TRAIL

"He replied, 'When evening comes, you say, "It will be fair weather, for the sky is red," and in the morning, "Today it will be stormy, for the sky is red and overcast." You know how to interpret the appearance of the sky, but you cannot interpret the signs of the times.'"

—Matthew 16:2–3

I spent nearly four years in Trump world—as the national spokesperson for the Republican National Committee, as the press secretary for the Trump campaign, and finally as White House press secretary. Every position came with its own set of circumstances— levels of notoriety and expectations for being in the Swamp. I can easily say that my most valued moments were not the moments that I walked to the White House podium, ready to face a room full of hostile correspondents. No, the time that meant the most to me was the time I spent at Trump rallies, with a microphone and a camera interviewing the men and women—marginalized and demonized— who made up the conservative movement.

Hillary Clinton called us "deplorable and irredeemable."[1]

Peter Strzok described us as "hillbillies" that he could "smell."[2]

CNN pundits went with "credulous rubes," asserting that we could not locate countries on a map.[3]

And President Joe Biden referred to those who preferred reopening the country "Neanderthal[s]."[4]

Nope.

The Trump voters I met were none of those things. During my time at the Trump campaign, I was pregnant with Blake. All throughout my pregnancy, I ventured out into the crowds at rallies. The People I met were incredible. There was the veteran who told me that President Trump literally saved his life. On the verge of suicide, he found hope and opportunity in a president who truly cared about veterans. On the evening that House Democrats impeached President Trump over a phone call, I met a young man who recounted that his life was forever changed by the Trump presidency. He received an unduly harsh sentence for a nonviolent offense, and President Trump's First Step Act meant that he got to be with his family for Christmas. And then there was the woman who ran up to me and prayed over my nine-month pregnant belly. Draped in a Trump flag, she gently placed her hand on my stomach, bowed her head, and said a prayer.

Yes, these are the men and women I know and love.

During my time on the campaign trail, it was an honor shaking hands with these patriots, hugging their necks, and hearing their stories. There were people from all walks of life and all different backgrounds. Listening to them prepared me for my time in the White House. The American People were on my mind when I stood at that podium.

When I worked on the campaign, I would usually fly in a day before the rally, go out the evening before, and interview the men and women camping out ahead of President Trump's rally. These voters intrigued me most. "*This is incredible*," I thought when I attended a rally in Green Bay, Wisconsin, in April of 2019. At this point, I had only been national press secretary for the Trump campaign for a short time. This was only the third Trump rally I had ever attended. I rushed off the plane to the rally venue the evening before the rally to do an interview on *Hannity*. When I arrived, I noticed a group of people with tents.

"*Are they camping out?*" I wondered.

At the conclusion of my interview, a woman came over to me and confirmed that they were all sleeping outside. Trump rallies always hit full capacity, often with an overflow crowd, and they wanted to ensure they had a spot.

"Would you please come meet a friend of mine who is camping out?" she asked me.

"Of course, I will."

As I approached the crowd of campers, I was amazed at what I saw. Holding American flags and bundled up in coats, these rally-goers were prepared to sleep overnight. I taped a short video with the crowd before meeting the gentleman I had initially gone to meet. He was a veteran who was hospitalized in the VA. He told me that he had called the veteran hotline that President Trump set up for veterans when they were receiving inadequate care. He didn't think he would hear back, but he did. In fact, he received a call directly from Lara Trump, President Trump's daughter-in-law. He told me that he was stunned by her personal outreach and her caring demeanor. "I'm alive today because of the great care I received," the man told me, crediting Trump for turning the VA around. I asked him to share his story on camera, and he ended by saying, "There's a lot of stories like this."

He was right. I heard stories like these and saw enthusiasm like this group's all over the country. After my pregnancy, I brought my daughter out on the campaign trail. My mom would babysit her in the hotel room, and I would go out to conduct "man on the street" interviews like these. We went everywhere—Iowa, South Carolina, North Carolina, and even New Jersey, a state often ignored by Republican presidents. I was curious what that Wildwood, New Jersey, rally would be like. It was a solidly blue state, and I wondered if the support would be more tepid. Boy, was I wrong!

"You have got to get out here now," one of the cameramen called to tell me. "There are more than a thousand people sleeping out. Not a hundred, a thousand—in forty-degree weather!"

I left Blake and my mom in the hotel room and ventured out into the cold. It was about midnight when I arrived at the venue, positioned just across from a motel. The motel had Trump banners in nearly every window, American flags draped as well. I was simply stunned at the throngs and throngs of people sleeping in this frigid weather. I set out with my microphone to find out why.

"My brother has to be in line, waiting seven years to come legally in this country and just today, he got the letter saying that he's going to be able to come here legally," one woman told me. "Seven years my brother was waiting…and the other people want to come jump in line and do everything wrong and get everything free and no working or anything…and I have to work and pay for that. I don't think so." I hugged the woman and congratulated her on her brother's great news. "Go Trump!" she finished.

Leaving the campaign, sadly, meant that I got to interact with these rallygoers far less. With my new job, I could no longer do these "man on the street" interviews, but I passed the mantle to a worthy successor. My twenty-five-year-old sister, Ryann, took over. Ryann is beautiful, relatable, and incredibly down-to-earth. There was no better person for the job. She would regularly and excitedly send these interviews to me. These videos kept me in check with the American People, even while in the White House.

Experiencing the campaign trail from the White House was an entirely distinct experience. First, the mode of transportation was just *a little* different. Instead of flying in a day or two before on a commercial airline, often having a stop on the way, and then flying back the day after the rally, I got to fly in and out on Air Force One. Before joining the White House, I had been on the light blue and white presidential aircraft a few times when there was an extra spot for a campaign person. I'll never forget my first journey in the "President's office in the sky."[5] A White House staffer took me under their wing, showing me how to use the telephone on the armrest. "You can call your family from the flight," they said. "It's pretty cool. The operator will call and say that they have received a call from Air Force One. You may want to warn them in advance, though. It's an odd set of numbers that appear on the phone."

I told my parents, husband, and in-laws to be prepared for a call from a number they might not recognize. When I boarded the plane, I eagerly called each one. "I'm so sorry," I said to the AF1 operator. "Just one more!" When my mom received her call, she went into panic mode. "Mike!" she said to my father. "Wake up! I think it's the president calling. You answer!" It was only me, but we got quite a laugh out of the confusion.

During that first trip on the plane, I got to go to the president's cabin and talk with him, Don Jr., Brad Parscale, and a few others. I didn't know the president well. We had spoken a few times, but this was really my first substantial in-person interaction, other than when he visited CNN on the campaign trail back in 2016 when I was a CNN political commentator. During that AF1 flight, as I sat with the president, I was admittedly a little nervous. From behind his brown, wooden presidential desk, President Trump watched Fox News for analysis of his rally or the day's news cycle. Seated around the perimeter of the room on a brown leather couch, those in the room watched in silence with him. During the commercial break, President Trump talked with Don, Brad, and me, often posing questions.

"What are your thoughts on that topic?" he asked me, interested in seeing what the newbie on board AF1 thought. I recognized his jesting and fun personality during that first interaction. Over the next year on the campaign trail, I would talk to him at each rally, at least for a few moments. I was often the last person he spoke to before heading onto the rally catwalk.

"Kayleigh, did you speak at this rally?" he would always ask. "I want you speaking at every rally as the warm-up." I was flattered at the president's confidence in me. He eventually pulled aside senior level campaign aides to make sure that I got an opportunity to address the crowd.

As cool as it was to interact with the president on that first AF1 trip, the biggest highlight of the voyage was that I was just a few weeks pregnant with my first child. My parents and in-laws did not know at the time, but when I took a picture in front of the navy "Aboard Air Force One" sign in the conference room on the plane, I knew it was far more special than just a picture of me. Blake was there, too, even though she was just a few weeks old in mommy's tummy. In fact, Blake would make a handful of trips on Air Force One while in my belly. She even flew on the plane eight days before she was born. Yes, eight days! During that trip, President Trump signed my "Aboard AF1" name placard with a gold sharpie: "Kayleigh, you are great," he wrote above his signature. Just over a week after that trip, my baby girl would be here.

"Well, at least if you give birth on the plane, the White House physicians will be there," Jared Kushner joked. I laughed, and secretly kind of hoped she would be. What a cool story that would be!

In the White House, my AF1 trips would become routine. That being said, they never lost their majesty. Each trip with the president seemed to bring a new and exciting experience. Like the first time I road in an MV-22 Osprey. An Osprey is a military aircraft with two rotors (propeller-like, spinning blades) on either side. At night, these rotors light up green, sending a bright neon green circle into the darkness. Used primarily for military operations, the Osprey is also used to transport White House personnel, Secret Service, and the press pool in the event that the destination is too far to travel to and from AF1 by motorcade. The interior of the aircraft has tons of exposed wiring and electrical work. What makes the Osprey unique is that it is not fully enclosed, even during flight!

I would load onto the Osprey via a loading ramp. The red and yellow carpeted ramp reads "HMX-1" standing for "Marine Helicopter Squadron One," the squadron that also flew Marine One.[6] I learned quickly that I had to be careful to hold down my dress upon boarding. The rotors generated a lot of wind and could very easily lift an A-line dress or a skirt. After loading, I took a seat as far away from the opening at the back of the aircraft as I could. During takeoff, the nose of the aircraft tilted upward and there seemed to be a pulling force toward the opening at the back of the aircraft. I grabbed the edges of my seat as tightly as I could.

But while I felt I was holding on for dear life, a marine positioned at the back hatch happily sat at the edge of the Osprey, even leaning forward a little into the opening as we neared landing, apparently unafraid at the thought of falling off the ledge. "*This is frightening,*" I kept thinking, even though I knew the marine was secured by a harness. As I flew on my first Osprey, I couldn't help but think about our heroic military men and women. I flew on this Osprey heading to a campaign rally or a presidential fundraiser after a glamorous flight on Air Force One; they flew on an Osprey heading into a war zone, a battle, or a high-stakes military operation. This Osprey was the last thing many of them saw before landing in a foreign country and hoping to come out alive.

As I took more Osprey trips, I got a little braver. When an Air Force pilot observed my interest in the Osprey, he asked if I wanted to sit near the edge—not where the marine hovered over the edge but in the nearest seat. "Yes," I cautiously agreed. Observing the marine sitting on the back of the aircraft, mere feet from a massive drop off, I said to her, "Wow. You are brave. Thank you for your service."

When we weren't taking an Osprey and Marine One to our destination, we would take a presidential motorcade from the tarmac to wherever we were heading. President Trump would ride in the Beast, his staff and press pool in vans behind him, escorted by a cadre of police. As we traveled the country, it was incredible watching the masses of people who would line the streets, usually with supportive signs. There were some protesters, too, but the support was overwhelming. October 18, 2020, was probably the biggest crowd I saw lining the streets to support President Trump. Like that New Jersey rally, this mass of supporters showed up in a blue state. Arriving in Orange County, California, the crowd stretched for at least a mile.[7]

Between at-capacity rallies and multitudes of supporters who would line the streets of the presidential motorcade, President Trump had created a political phenomenon. As his campaign press secretary, I saw how he connected with the crowds during these events. As his White House press secretary, I also saw how his loyalty to his voters was not just an act. The Trump supporters camping out the night before a rally or standing in a ridiculously long line the day of, recognized a boldness in President Trump, but they also saw authenticity. He was so clearly not a politician, but rather someone willing to speak the truth and follow through. The loyalty of his supporters was met by a reciprocated loyalty from a commander in chief.

I'll never forget a meeting that we had on June 22, 2020, in the Cabinet Room at the White House. The president sat at the center of an enormous mahogany table. The chairs around the table each had placards denoting the respective departments they represented. This meeting, however, was not a Cabinet meeting. It was a meeting with the president and his advisors, including Attorney General Bill Barr, to determine if the administration would file a brief in support of states that were challenging the legality of the Affordable Care Act (Obamacare). While Brooke Rollins, a White House aide and soon-to-be director of the Domestic Policy Council, advocated strongly for the president to continue fighting Obamacare in court, others did not.

Attorney General Bill Barr made a strong case for getting out of the lawsuit, as did Kellyanne Conway. We were in the middle of the COVID-19 outbreak, and it didn't seem to be the right time to target a healthcare program—however costly and counterproductive Obamacare may be in the long-run. Moreover, there was absolutely no doubt that Democrats would use our participation in the lawsuit as a political cudgel. Oral arguments were scheduled right around election time, and Democrats would use this as a weapon.

Listening to the back and forth, the president pressed his aides on the matter. Then he looked at me and said, "Kayleigh, what do you think?"

"Mr. President," I said. "I have to agree with Kellyanne and the Attorney General. I think there are a lot of risks here."

He listened to what I had to say and then uttered that sentiment I will never forget. President Trump said something to the effect of: "I don't care. I will stand with my base and the promises I made to them," referring to the fact that he would rather lose support than go back on his word.

In that moment, I realized the authenticity of the president. This, to me, felt like political suicide. But his unflinching loyalty to the voters who put him there, and most of all, his "promises made, promises kept" demeanor is what mattered to him most.

❦

THE CAMPAIGN TRAIL WAS, no doubt, rigorous at times, but it was also a lot of fun. President Trump always made sure of that. He also made sure that I was always on my toes. While he spoke on a Minnesota tarmac in August, he randomly said, "Kayleigh, come say a few words." Fortunately, I was well-versed in Operation Legend, the Trump administration-led effort to get violent criminals off the street. My points matched the president's law-and-order-centric speech. The call-ups or call-outs became somewhat of a trend.

During a roundtable in Iowa about the devastating windstorms (called derechos) that had ravaged the area, President Trump called on me to make a few remarks. From Iowa derechos to law and order in Minnesota, I had to always be prepared. At a rally in Prescott, Arizona, as I huddled in a tent for staff behind the outdoor rally set-up, I randomly heard the president say, "Kayleigh, where's Kayleigh? Is she here? Our great Kayleigh. Where's Kayleigh? Kayleigh?"

I quickly threw down my phone and ran toward the stage in my beige patent leather heels before appearing at the edge of the catwalk. He was looking around when he saw me and motioned for me to come on stage.

"Come here, Kayleigh," he said, as he started clapping with the crowd.

After a short walk, I joined him on stage in my red, A-line dress.

"So she just recovered from COVID. Can you believe it?" he said before joking, "Stay away from me Kayleigh. Stay away." He then gave me the microphone for a moment. "Say a couple words."

"Let me tell you guys," I said. "With your help, we can beat social media. We can beat the media because we have the greatest fighter in the history of this country in President Donald J. Trump."

The crowded applauded as I left the stage. "Thank you. She is so great. She is so great," he emphasized. "I didn't know she would be that good. That was good…. You know, she's married to a professional Major League Baseball player."

That Prescott, Arizona, rally came in the final weeks of the campaign. The schedule ahead was daunting. We had thirty-five rallies left on the schedule—in just two weeks. The final days on the trail, in particular, would be exhausting—five rallies in one day.

Yes, FIVE—and all in different states!

The president's humorous demeanor and the good group of senior staff who traveled with him made the arduous schedule a lot easier.

In those final days on the trail, a core of senior staff took to the road with the president—Mark Meadows, Jared Kushner, Dan Scavino, Hope Hicks, Stephen Miller, Derek Lyons, and me. At the end of each rally, President Trump—a careful curator of the rally playlist—had decided that the "Y.M.C.A." would be his walk-off song. Along with his new exit tune came a new dance move. Stopping somewhere along the catwalk, he would peer into the crowd and do a little jig. It was absolutely hilarious. The staff always watched for the moment. But after watching the president dance on stage, I thought at one September rally, *"How can we not be dancing to the 'Y.M.C.A.' too?"*

"You know what, I'm going to go for *it*," I said to myself, stretching my hands up to form a "Y", cupping them in the air for the "M", over to the left for the "C", and then coming to a point back up top for the "A." I noticed the press looking over at me. "*Whatever,*" I thought. When I got back to DC, a staffer sent me a note: "HAHAHA the pool report!!!" The pool report was a product put together by the traveling press pool. They wrote out noteworthy descriptions about the president's trip that other reporters might want to use in their reporting.

This pool report read: "One last extremely important note: colleagues informed your pooler that the president's grandchildren and the press secretary were doing the 'YMCA' as the Village People song played when POTUS left the stage in Moon Township. Your pooler did not personally witness this, but we would be remiss if we didn't include the detail. You can do whatever you feel."[8]

It was a dig, from a snarky reporter. But who cared? I was the press secretary, yes. But I'm also a fun-loving human. Bringing some lightness to a tough job was something I relished. As the days progressed, I slowly got others to partake in the "Y.M.C.A." dancing. Will Russell, deputy director of presidential advance operations and trip director, was among the first to join along with Johnny McEntee. Eventually, I enlisted soon-to-be chief of staff for the Department of Defense, Kash Patel. I remember Ivanka playfully trolling Jared for not joining in the fun.

At a late October rally in The Villages in Florida, the president observed my "Y.M.C.A." dancing offstage. "Come on," he said, as he motioned for me to join him on the catwalk. I ascended the stairs and accompanied him on his exit walk, dancing to the "Y.M.C.A." in my rainbow-trimmed dress. I was having so much fun in The Villages that I accidentally left my purse—yes, my purse—at the rally. I only realized it after I boarded the Osprey to head back to Air Force One. Fortunately, a campaign staffer was able to recover it and give it to me at a rally the next day in a different state.

After rallies, President Trump loved coming back and convening with senior staff and guests on the plane. Sometimes, he would sit and talk for extended periods of time. I remember him sitting with us after a rally just days before the election. Minority Leader Kevin McCarthy was there. The president ordered everyone at the table orange soda. After another rally in late October, he came to the conference room for about thirty minutes and sat down and ate cookies with us. During that trip, it was game four of the World Series, and he knew that my husband was a pitcher traveling with the Tampa Bay Rays. For Sean, this wasn't his first time at Major League Baseball's championship series. He had been with the New York Mets in 2015, when the team battled through playoffs before ultimately facing the Kansas City Royals. Sean actually got to pitch in that one! As the senior White House staff watched the 2020 World Series aboard AF1, the president started asking about Sean. "I want to see him pitch," he said.

Game four ended up being a crazy one. The Dodgers had won two games, the Rays one. This game offered a chance to tie it up, but that didn't look likely. The Rays were down, seven to six. They had tied it up in the sixth inning before falling behind. By the ninth inning, the Rays were behind by one run. I watched each hitter with bated breath. Though one player got on base, hope slowly faded as the Dodgers got two outs, two strikes. "This will be the last pitch," Mark Meadows said. He was right, though not in the way we all had envisioned.

Since I know next to nothing about baseball, I asked my husband to insert a description of the play in the following paragraph. For those who know as little about baseball as me, please bear with me as I provide my husband the opportunity to write a brief description. Don't shut this book just yet.

Down to their last strike with two men on base, the Rays were about to find themselves unlikely victors. Brett Phillips took Kenley Jansen's one-two cutter and promptly lined it into short right field for a base hit. That hit alone would have tied the game, but Dodger center fielder Chris Taylor bobbled the ball, allowing for the impending craziness to ensue. The costly error would not only allow Phillips an opportunity to get to second, but it would also allow Randy Arozarena, who was the runner on first, an opportunity to try and score. When Taylor bobbled the ball in short center, Randy had already rounded second base and was heading for third. Forcing the Dodgers to make two perfect throws to get him out at the plate, he rounded third. Halfway from scoring, he trips and barrel rolls. Quickly rising to his feet, he tried to get back to third, but soon realized he was closer to home than to third. So, he changed his direction yet again and tried to make what at this point looked like a feeble attempt at scoring the winning run. The relay throw from Taylor to first baseman Max Muncy was a decent one, and it looked like the Dodgers had Arozarena dead to rights. But Muncy's short toss to catcher Will Smith was up the line and caused Smith to reach around to his left, taking his momentum away from the play at the plate. Trying to make a quick catch and sweep tag all in one motion, Smith dropped the ball and allowed Arozarena the chance to score.

Thank you, Sean, for that. Now, I've taken back the keyboard, and if you are as confused as I am, all you need to know is that it was the wildest baseball play I have ever seen!

That night, cheering broke out aboard Air Force One as we all reflected on just how crazy that play actually was. We were jubilant. I deplaned, and one reporter said to me, "We were watching the game, and cheering for the Rays." Sports could always provide a moment of unity, especially as the nation continued to suffer through COVID.

By the time election eve arrived, our traveling senior staff group felt like a small family. When we boarded Air Force One that morning, the mood was a jocular one. Stephen Miller, senior advisor for policy and director of speechwriting, was notorious for teasing me during our long flights. Election eve was no exception.

"Kayleigh, did you know that shrimp are mentioned in the Bible?" he asked me in an inquiring tone.

"Come on, Stephen," I laughed. "I'm gullible, but I'm not that gullible."

"I'm not joking. I'm serious. I can't believe you don't know this," he said with seriousness.

"Mark," I said, directing the conversation to the chief of staff, who I knew to be a well-studied man of faith. "Stephen says that 'shrimp' are mentioned in the Bible. I'm not buying it."

"I think he's right," Mark confirmed. "Shell creatures are mentioned."

This prompted a nearly ten-minute debate on whether the crustacean was indeed mentioned. That was until National Security Advisor Robert O'Brien said he had found the answer. Reading Leviticus out loud as we all sat around the table, he quoted, "Of all the creatures living in the water of the seas and the streams you may eat any that have fins and scales. But all the creatures in the seas or streams that do not have fins and scales—whether among all the swarming things or among all the other living creatures in the water—you are to regard as unclean—Leviticus 11: 9–10."[9]

"I told you," Stephen gloated.

"I didn't just hear the word 'shrimp,'" I implored, unwilling to lose an argument.

We laughed about the debate throughout the day. It was emblematic of our banter aboard Air Force One.

On that final day on the campaign trail, we landed in Traverse City, Michigan, for our third of five rallies to one of the most beautiful sunsets I had ever seen, and that is saying a lot from a Florida girl. Yellow, orange, purple, and even red filled the crisp fall sky. It was something to behold. As I stood on that tarmac gazing at the sky, a close friend of mine and spiritual mentor texted me, "I have no clue what's to come—but the verse I got for you tonight is 1 Corinthians 2:9 'That is what the Scriptures mean when they say, "No eye has seen, no ear has heard, and no mind has imagined what God has prepared for those who love him."'" No matter what, Christ was in control.

That stunning November sky in Michigan prompted someone to mention Matthew 16:2–3 to me. I looked it up. It was the words of Jesus Christ to the Pharisees and Sadducees—the privileged religious leaders who thought *they* were the authorities and not the humble but all-powerful Christ who stood before them. The Pharisees and Sadducees had come to Jesus to "test him" and "show them a sign from heaven."[10] Jesus said, "When it is evening, you say, 'It will be fair weather, for the sky is red.' And in the morning, 'It will be stormy today, for the sky is red and threatening.' You know how to interpret the appearance of the sky, but you cannot interpret the signs of the times." As the Jeremiah Study Bible notes, "Ironically, Jesus Himself was the sign from heaven...."[11] But the religious leaders had missed it.

This verse became the impetus for a common expression among mariners: "Red sky at night, sailors' delight; red sky at morning, sailors take warning."[12] Though we had a red sky in Michigan that evening, no one could predict what was to come, and no sign was necessary. For the "sign from heaven," Jesus Christ, was in control.

CHAPTER 12

BABY BLAKE

"Someday when the pages of my life end, I know that you will be one of the most beautiful chapters."

—Unknown

I woke up on Sunday, October 25, 2020, totally and completely exhausted. I had been on the campaign trail for seven days straight—ten different rallies in eight different states. We had spent a few nights on the road, and I just wanted to spend the day with my eleven-month-old daughter in my DC apartment. That morning we watched *Puppy Dog Pals* together and danced to the song she so loved.

As the morning progressed, I tried two different Halloween outfits on Blake—one light pink fairy outfit and another darker pink Sleeping Beauty outfit. She looked so cute. It was hard to choose! I knew our time was dwindling. I would soon need to head to the White House and get in the motorcade's support van en route to New Hampshire and then to Maine.

Having maximized my time with Blake to the last possible minute, I left my apartment in a panic, afraid I was going to miss the motorcade. Making matters worse, it was pouring rain outside. I ran through the rain, completely out of breath by the time I arrived at the motorcade. I had not missed my ride, but part of me wished I had. As I sat in a line of cars, waiting for the president to get in the Beast so we could head to Joint Base Andrews where Air Force One was waiting, I thought about getting out of the van.

"*I can just send someone else from the press staff,*" I rationalized. "*Just get out of the van, and you can spend the whole day with Blake.*"

But I knew I needed to be there. I promised myself that I would go on every trip leading up to the election. In just seven days, America would vote. I had to power through. Besides, that night the president was hosting Halloween at the White House, where he and the First Lady would greet children—including my daughter, Blake—on the White House lawn. This would be a quick trip, landing in New Hampshire, then heading to Maine, and then back to Washington.

As it turns out, this trip ended up being one of the most beautiful and unique trips I took with President Trump. Unlike the typical packed-out rallies, our final stop would be a surprise visit to the Treworgy Family Orchards in Levant, Maine. We motorcaded through Maine that afternoon, and I could not believe the stunning, bucolic images right outside my window. Cozy homes sat upon rolling green grass. The green leaves of the trees had turned to their warm fall hues—yellow, orange, and red. When we arrived at the orchard, I stood back as the president met the owners of the family farm.

"Kayleigh," he said. "Come here."

I walked up to the president.

"This lady is a big fan of yours," he noted. "She asked, 'Is that Kayleigh McEnany?' when I greeted her. Then she said, 'She's so smart and organized and does research.'"

I shook the sweet woman's hand, so flattered that she would share these words with my boss.

Since the event was announced just a few hours before the president's arrival, we did not expect a big crowd. It would be an intimate event, we thought. We were wrong. To our surprise, thousands had gathered. Standing behind crates of pumpkins and below an American flag, throngs of onlookers cheered as President Trump walked out.

"USA. USA," they shouted just before the president grabbed a bullhorn to thank the crowd for coming. Both the president and I walked the line of people, hearing their stories, shaking their hands, and looking them in the eye. It reminded me of when I interviewed rallygoers during my time as campaign press secretary. But this time I got to interact with the people right alongside the president—a true honor. Walking along the line, I met a mom standing just behind a little girl in a pink jacket. I knelt down and gave the girl a big hug, her hot pink jacket grazing my light pink scarf. But I had another little girl waiting at home, my little girl, dressed in her pink Halloween costume and waiting for Mommy.

When we boarded AF1, the staff talked about what a raving success the event was. As the AF1 crew served us a delicious pasta with seasonal pumpkin sauce, Dave Bossie, a close campaign aide to the president, worked feverishly to try to rework the president's schedule for the final days on the campaign trail. We all agreed that we needed more retail politics stops like that surprise visit to the orchard. A little way into the trip, President Trump came and sat with us in the conference room. Someone had thought to pick up pumpkin donuts during our time at the orchard. A great move. We reflected on the event with the president and enjoyed our pumpkin donuts. During the visit to the orchard, the president had greeted a few commercial fishermen in the rope line. With his bullhorn amplifying his voice, he mentioned that he had provided these fishermen in Maine with more opportunity by allowing commercial fishing in a conservation area.[1] On the plane he said to me, "These guys ask for nothing. They just want to work. That's it." He cared.

We touched down at Joint Base Andrews and loaded into the motorcade. I gazed out the window of the van, pleased to be on the final leg of my journey to see Baby Blake. Dressed up in her pink costume, Blake was waiting in the White House with my mom, ready for the Halloween festivities. When the motorcade pulled into the White House, I darted to my office as quickly as I could. My mom, Lyndee, and Chad were all there as Blake crawled along my office's navy blue carpet with imprinted beige flowers. I made sure Blake's headband was secure, picked her up, and walked out to the West Wing Colonnade. We encountered a White House photographer along the way who snapped a mommy-daughter picture. I was finally back with my little girl.

⚬⚬⚬

LIKE MANY WORKING MOMS, I have come to know the tensions between family and work all too well. On that October day, like many other days during my time in the White House and on the campaign, the career I loved and the family I loved even more were on a collision course. It's a tension that I felt my whole adult life. As a determined young woman, I set out to forge a career in media and politics at the highest level. But even more than dreams of pursuing a career, I had a burning desire to be a wife and a mother.

To be a wife, however, I would need to find a husband, and as any woman in our current day and age knows, that can be quite a challenge. When I started law school at twenty-five years old, I had been through my fair share of heartbreak. That's why I decided to devote myself entirely to school. I was emotionally exhausted, and rather than seeking a man, I wanted to focus on me. As any law student knows, the first year of law school—known as "1L year"—is the most challenging. It is a year of rigor, work, and pure devotion to academics. As I mentioned previously, I ended my first year of law school at Miami with the highest grades in my class. I still hadn't found a husband, or even a boyfriend for that matter, but for the moment, I did not mind. I was proud of my accomplishment.

I spent my second year of law school at Harvard primarily focused on my studies, but by the spring of 2015, I was headed to New York City for a summer associate position at a law firm, and I was ready to reenter the dating world—on my terms. My life changed when I came across the Twitter profile of Sean Gilmartin, a left-handed pitcher on the New York Mets. Fully clad in camouflage in his Twitter profile picture, Sean was unlike any man I had met in New York, but, I would soon find, a lot like the man I looked up to—my father. After inspecting his profile and seeing no red flags, I decided to message him. Why not?

"Hey! I see you like to hunt & fish – that is rare in NYC! haha," I messaged him. "Nice to see someone who appreciates the southern way of life up here. Are you from the South?" We began to message back and forth and eventually met for some New York-style Southern food at Southern Hospitality. He will never let me forget that I got spicy shrimp all in my hair during our first dinner. The rest was history!

But as we dated, my career and our new budding relationship began to intersect. One night, we had plans to bake a pizza and then head to a movie. Sean was pulling the pizza out of the oven when I got a call from CNN, asking me to join Don Lemon on *CNN Tonight*. I had appeared on CNN a few years earlier. It had been a while, though, so the call was a bit of a surprise. The 2016 primaries had just begun, and CNN was in need of at least a few conservative voices, which is why they called me. I was excited at the opportunity to share my perspective on the 2016 primaries, but a little torn as Sean's and my relationship was new, and I didn't want to break our plans.

"I know this seems crazy," I told him. "But this is how the world of television works. I have an idea. Why don't you come with me?" In a show of support, he agreed to come, and we left his New Jersey apartment, rushed into New York City, and headed into CNN's studios. My appearances on CNN grew to be more regular as our relationship proceeded. The summer of 2015 became a summer of baseball, television, and young love. On many occasions, I would leave my law firm and head to Citi Field, home to the New York Mets. I would pick up my ticket at player will call and sit in the family section of the stadium. Watching Sean pitch in the warm summer air with an ice-cold beer became a favorite activity. Some days it was relaxing. Other days it was interspersed with calls from producers, asking for talking points.

Summer turned to fall, and both of our careers grew. Sean and the Mets made their way to the World Series. I, meanwhile, went back to Cambridge, Massachusetts, for my final year of law school. I also secured spots on coveted presidential primary night and debate night panels on CNN before ultimately getting a contract with the network. But all of this meant sacrifice. Being away from Sean after a summer together was difficult, but we both understood one another's careers and supported each other's ambitions. I had found a supportive boyfriend and a good man who would ultimately become my husband.

During the first few years of our marriage, our long distance and traveling continued. Sean joined a number of baseball teams in different states, and I moved to work in politics in DC, even though our home was in Florida. Despite the challenges, as people of faith and supportive spouses, we found a way to embrace the situation, and we didn't let either of our jobs get in the way of our desire to have a family.

In the spring of 2019, I had landed a new job as national press secretary for the Trump campaign. I knew that I had two years of rigor ahead, working in this key job on a national campaign, so I thought, *"What better time to have a child than now?"* The reality is there is no absolutely *perfect* time to have a child, so why let the challenges of my job stand in the way? We decided to have our first child, and I was blessed to get pregnant just before my thirtieth birthday.

I spent my pregnancy traveling the country to rallies and political events. My stomach continued to grow, and I was truly grateful to have an easy and even energetic pregnancy. Blake flew all across the nation before arriving that November. As any parent will tell you, the love you have for your child is a new love that you have never experienced. Baby Blake filled our hearts with joy and blessed the Christmas season for her new parents.

But as New Year's came, I knew that my time in Florida was coming to an end, and that meant my time with Blake was going to change. I had already experienced what it was like to leave her at home. A few weeks after giving birth, I had traveled to rallies in Hershey, Pennsylvania, and Battle Creek, Michigan. I didn't want to miss a beat on the job, but as exhilarating as these rallies were, nothing could compare to time with my newborn.

New Year's Eve approached and worrying over how I would achieve this work-mom balance became an obsession. My husband and dad were on a hunting trip, so my mom and I decided to travel down to Miami to ring in the New Year with my grandmother, Mema. We knew she was getting older, and we wanted her to meet her new great-granddaughter. Ringing in the year 2020, we had the time of our lives, eating at a fancy Italian restaurant and prodding Mema to ditch her walker. My ninety-three-year-old grandmother had the heart of a child and the vitality of a teenager. We laughed as she sat on the walker, and we glided her through the streets of Miami—Mema on her walker and Blake in her stroller.

It was a perfect evening followed by an emotional morning. On January 1, 2020, reality set in. It would soon be time for me to head back to Washington, DC. I had printed a calendar and laid out all of my obligations—rallies in Ohio, Wisconsin, New Jersey, and Iowa plus a Women for Trump bus tour through Iowa. My eyes welled up with tears as I showed my mom my schedule.

"When will I ever see Blake?" I asked her.

She assured me that I would see my daughter, promising me that she would travel on the campaign trail and bring Blake. And she did just that. My amazing mother, Leanne, flew with me all across the country. Together, we dismantled massive strollers before going through security and then again before boarding the plane. We lugged Pack 'n Plays to the check-in counter and assembled a makeshift baby area in hotel rooms.

Every step of the way, the Trump family showed their support for me as a working mom. My mother and daughter got to fly on the campaign plane back from the Iowa caucus. Don Jr. offered to hold Baby Blake as Lara Trump looked on, holding her pacifier that had fallen to the floor. Todd Ricketts, the RNC finance chair, took over when Blake began to cry, rocking her to sleep before landing. It took a village, but we made it work during Blake's early days.

Just two months after that trip, and in the early days of COVID-19's onset, I would be taking my challenges of being a working mom to the White House. With all the trials accompanying my new job, working in the White House also brought quite a bit of fun and a whole lot of memories for Baby Blake.

⌒⌐⌐⌐⌐⌐⌐⌐⌐○

BEFORE STARTING AS WHITE House press secretary, I spoke with a few press secretaries who came before me, including Sarah Sanders. Sarah was the first mom to take to the podium. Following in her footsteps, I would also face the same challenges. "There will be times when he calls you and your kids will be screaming in the background. Don't worry. That's just part of being a working mom in the White House," she advised. She was right.

I remember one of the first times this happened. I decided to make a quick forty-eight-hour weekend trip down to the Florida Keys for mini lobster season—a family tradition. My service was spotty. My baby was screaming. And, of course, the president called.

"Oh my gosh, Mom. What do I do?" I asked her, sitting alongside Blake in the backseat. "It's the president!"

"Put on *Frozen*," she replied. "Quick!"

Holding a tablet in front of Blake, I started the movie *Frozen* as the president asked my advice on a list of upcoming interviews. I'm fairly certain he heard the well-known "Let It Go" lyrics belting out in the background!

Those weekend trips home kept me going, and my mom continued to bring Blake up to DC. In a way, the job in the White House, as compared to the campaign, made the logistics of spending time with Blake easier. Instead of flying across the country on commercial flights and setting up nurseries in hotels, for the most part, working in the White House meant that I returned to DC almost every night, albeit very late at times.

I seized on these little breaks in my DC apartment between rallies. My sister, Ryann, lived with me, and my mom often came up to the nation's capital with Blake. The McEnany women had a lot of fun during what little DC downtime we had. There was the time that I only brought one sock to work. Freaking out about what to do, my assistant brought me a pair of stockings she had. I cut the foot off the stocking to use as a second sock. Whatever…it would work. When I took off my boots upon arriving back at the apartment, my mom laughed as I displayed one black sock and another footsie stocking.

"You're the White House press secretary!" she exclaimed.

I may look like I have it all together. But rest assured, I do not! Going to an all-girls Catholic school meant that you would be lucky if I had showered back in my high school days, much less have matching socks!

These moments of levity at home were accompanied by frequent Baby Blake and family visits to the White House. Blake crawled on the floor of my office and through the grand White House center hall beneath the residence. She helped Mommy flip the pages of her briefing binder, sitting atop my desk. No doubt pictures that she will one day cherish.

Along the way, President Trump made my life as a working mom and a working wife easier. He regularly inquired about my family and my husband's baseball career. In July, Hall of Fame pitcher Mariano Rivera had come to the White House to mark Opening Day of Major League Baseball, a little later than usual due to COVID-19. A few days after Mariano's visit, President Trump visited the Red Cross—just across the street from the White House—to promote convalescent plasma, a COVID therapeutic. As we exited the building and walked toward the motorcade, the president motioned for me to come over.

"Join me in the Beast," he said.

What an honor. It was the first time I had ever seen or sat in the well-known, armored presidential vehicle.

We took the short journey across the street and into the White House gates while President Trump asked about my husband's baseball career. I told him that he was a relief pitcher, prompting the president to launch into a play-by-play recount of a Yankees game he had seen back in the day.

"The Sandman. The Sandman!" he kept saying.

"*Who the heck is this 'Sandman'?*" I thought.

"Is your husband impressed the Sandman came to the White House?" he asked.

When I got back to my office, I called my husband. He explained the "Sandman" was the nickname for Mariano Rivera, a reference to Metallica's song "Enter Sandman" that Rivera used as his walk-out song.

"Oh…that makes sense!" I told my husband.

I finally understood.

A few months later, in September, President Trump and I were about to walk out of the Diplomatic Room to board Marine One, heading to Air Force One to take off for a rally in Fayetteville, North Carolina. I spoke to the president briefly, and then he stepped out the door to take a few questions from the press. As he spoke, I waved to Baby Blake, standing just beyond the president and the press. Blake, my mom, and my aunts had all come to watch the president and me walk toward Marine One that Saturday afternoon. After taking some questions, he journeyed across the lawn, heading for the green helicopter that awaited him. I trailed behind.

The president saluted the marine and boarded the staircase on the left of the aircraft. A few other senior staffers and I boarded the staircase on the right. When I got on the helicopter, I headed toward where the president was sitting and sat on the bench right across from his chair. As we ascended from the South Lawn and into the DC sky, the president looked at me and asked, "Why are you here?"

"What? Why would he ask that?" I thought.

"Because I'm your press secretary and it's my job to be here," I said after a brief pause.

"No, I know that," he said. "And I'm glad you're here, but it's Saturday night. You could have sent one of the young kids who work for you. Where is your family tonight?"

"Well," I began. "My husband is currently with the Tampa Bay Rays, and they have a game tonight."

"Wow," he said in bewilderment. "He could pitch tonight."

Then the president turned back toward the rest of those on board and announced, "Kayleigh's husband is pitching tonight, and she chose to come a Trump rally. The greatest show on earth." He smiled and turned back to me.

On Air Force One, the president announced it again to a room full of people. "Kayleigh's husband is pitching tonight, and she chose to come to the Trump rally."

Throughout the night, the president kept asking how Sean was doing. I told him that Sean was active on the roster, and the Rays were playing the Baltimore Orioles. As a reliever, he could be called to pitch at any moment, but nothing was certain. I monitored the game and gave the president regular updates.

After the rally, I boarded Marine One with the president again to head back to the White House. "Kayleigh, it's a really impressive thing to get to the major leagues," he commented. "You have to have real talent. That's very hard to do and impressive."

I nodded and said, "That's true," beaming with pride at the amazing feat my husband had accomplished and proud that he was receiving a high compliment like this from the leader of the free world.

"Go watch your husband," the president said. "That's important."

As we landed on the White House lawn, the president wrapped up the evening with this: "You know what. You go sit in the back Oval dining room. Turn on the game. Watch your husband."

"That's so nice of you to offer," I said.

"No, I mean it. Go to my back Oval Office and enjoy the game," he insisted before getting off Marine One and walking back to his private residence.

I didn't take the president up on his very generous offer, but it meant a lot that he would make an offer like that, and it meant even more that he spent the night inquiring about my husband and encouraging me to spend time with family.

And it wasn't just the president who made my work-life balance easier. In the early days of my time in the Trump administration, I wasn't sure what my schedule would be like. On the campaign, in those early days of 2020, I would try and take weekends to be home in Florida with my family, but I imagined that there would be no time for this in the White House. I assumed people went to the office seven days a week, but I wasn't sure. So, I spent the first few weekends as press secretary in Washington, DC, away from my family.

On Friday, May 8th, I finally felt comfortable enough to leave the Swamp and head home to Florida, but I would have to get through a White House press briefing first. The briefing was incredibly stressful as I learned several hours before that Katie Miller, the vice president's press secretary and Stephen Miller's wife, had tested positive for COVID-19. This unexpected news would surely dominate the briefing. We scrambled on that Friday afternoon, but the light at the end of the tunnel was the flight I had booked to go home to Florida and see Blake and Sean.

After the briefing and at the very last minute, though, my staff encouraged me to stay and attend an event that President Trump was hosting with Republican members of Congress. My heart sank. I wanted to go home and be with my family, but I also wanted to do a good job as press secretary. I was torn, but I reluctantly agreed to stay back and attend the event. I canceled my flight before walking across the West Wing Colonnade and toward the State Dining Room.

When I arrived at the event, the president was sitting at the center of a rectangular seating arrangement, surrounded by Republican members of Congress. I walked toward the back left of the room to find my seat as the president looked at me and announced to the attendees, "We were just talking about you! Tell the congressmen about the polling you mentioned to me." After I finished speaking, he asked me to hold up my notes for all of them to see. I finally took my seat when I saw the chief of staff walking in my direction.

"Why are you here?" Mark whispered to me. "Shouldn't you be on a flight?"

"Yes, but I thought it was important I be here," I responded.

"No," he said, shaking his head. "Go home and be with your family. That is most important. Now get to that flight."

I quickly ran back to my office, rebooked my flight, and spent a much-needed weekend with my family before heading back to DC to return to work. The president and the chief of staff's prioritization of family made my once-in-a-lifetime experience that much better because I did not have to sacrifice being a mom to my daughter.

THOSE LAST DAYS ON the campaign trail were exhausting but rewarding. Three days before the election, I woke up at 5:30 a.m. to do a television hit on *Fox & Friends* followed by six other local

Florida television appearances. We were overnighting at Doral in Miami, Florida, and I had a late night followed by an early morning. I was wiped out as I got in the car to head to the studio for my morning TV hit, but the fatigue could not overcome the excitement I felt for what was ahead. We were about to load onto Air Force One and head to a rally in my hometown in Tampa, Florida. The Trump rally was coming to Tampa, and my whole family would be there.

I arrived at my early morning hit, and we had big-time audio problems. The studio technician rushed to program audio through my iPhone. I had no clue how this was going to work. When I finally got on the air, the audio problems had not resolved. Instead of no audio, I had two audio feeds—one in real time and another on a seven-second delay. As I spoke to Ainsley, Steve, and Brian, I could hear my voice and theirs on a seven-second delay. It was an unimaginably difficult scenario, but I made my way through the hit.

When I got back to my hotel room, I noticed a missed call from the president. I called him back. "Kayleigh, that was a great hit on *Fox & Friends*," he said. "I loved what you said on COVID. Call Stephen Miller and get this in my speech. I want to play it on the big screens."

At the president's rallies, the campaign had started streaming short snippets of commentators on topics important to that area of the country. In Allentown, Pennsylvania, for example, he played a video of Joe Biden praising China and hitting fracking. I assumed my clip would just be one of many in the videos he would play in Tampa. I was honored.

Aboard AF1, President Trump told me two more times how impressed he was with my hit. Maybe the two audio feeds were a good luck charm?

The flight was a short one, flying just north from Miami to Tampa. We got to Tampa International Airport and took a short motorcade ride to an outside venue overlooking Raymond James Stadium, home to the Tampa Bay Bucs. When we got there, President Trump and the First Lady walked on stage together. I followed alongside the catwalk on the grass in my bright purple dress, clapping and cheering with the rest of the crowd. When we got closer to the stage, I looked behind me, and there were Sean and Blake!

Sean was wearing a navy blue T-shirt with my face on it. Near the end of the campaign season, someone had designed paraphernalia with my image. Cast in the colors of red and blue, a picture of me at the podium had been turned into an illustration. Beneath my face read the word "FACTS." I saw these shirts pop up at rallies throughout the campaign, and I was honored that my husband thought to wear his that day.

He was holding Blake. She was wearing a light blue and white checkered romper with lemons. I gave them both a hug, and we embraced as the president's walk-on song, "I'm Proud to be an American," played. My parents were sitting near the front of the stage, and my in-laws were helping with Blake backstage. "*Wow. This is truly incredible*," I thought. "*I am home!*" The rally began, and I introduced my family to Jared, Mark, and the whole team.

Tampa brought a euphoric crowd in a very hot environment—so hot that at one point massive sprinklers showered the back of the crowd with water. "Look at that," the president said from the stage. "Oh, are they doing that on purpose?"

"Are they friend or foe? I don't know. Actually, it felt good," he said. Even he could feel the light mist. "I felt water on my face. I said, 'Where the hell is that coming from?' They may be doing that on purpose. Let's find out if they're friend or foe!"

"Friend or foe," he shouted, as I laughed from the sidelines.

About midway through, I heard the president say, "I just want to play you a video…. I was so impressed. It's a little bit. We only do this for people that we love. We have these very expensive boards that come along, and this is largely a woman that comes from this area."

I heard his reference to me as my husband, Blake, and I stood just off the side of the stage.

"Her husband happens to be a Major League Baseball player," he continued. "Do you know who I'm talking about?"

Shouts of "Kayleigh" rang out from my hometown crowd.

"He's a handsome guy, but she's far more beautiful, and he's on Tampa Bay, so he's right now a little depressed," the president noted, referring to the fact that the Rays had just lost the World Series. "I don't know if he's here or not, but if he is, I want to talk to him and say you did a great job. Kayleigh, please come up here, Kayleigh, and play the video, please. Play the video."

Soon after the president called for it, my *Fox & Friends* appearance from that morning popped on the screen. "As the *New York Post* noted today, this is a mob artist," I said in the appearance, referring to Twitter CEO Jack Dorsey's decision to censor the Hunter Biden story. "This is a shakedown effort to say, 'Delete the Hunter Biden story. The media won't report on it. Social media will censor it. Delete it [they say], or we will censor the fourth largest newspaper in the United States.'" At this point, I joined him on the stage, smiling as he clapped and welcomed me. My clip continued as the topic transitioned to COVID.

"The American people have a very clear choice when it comes to COVID," I said in the video. "You can vote [for] Joe Biden [and] you will be locked down. Your schools will be closed. Your churches will be closed. You won't have social gatherings. It will be a lockdown versus President Trump, where we are safely reopening this country. Americans deserve jobs. They deserve freedom. Joe Biden's modeling his strategy, which is lockdown in the basement."

"*How long was the clip?*" I wondered. I thought this was just going to be a snippet, but the president decided to play nearly three minutes of my appearance. As the clip was playing, the president asked me, "Is your husband here?"

"Yes," I said, pointing to him just off stage.

"Bring him up," he said, as I motioned for Sean and Blake to join me.

At the end of the clip, the president said to the crowd, "I mean, who's going to say it better than Kayleigh? So I want to congratulate you. This is our great looking couple. We almost had the Dodgers. Are they that good a team? They're pretty good, right?"

Sean nodded and mouthed, "They were good."

"Well, you're pretty good too, and you're a great couple, and that's a beautiful baby. Thank you very much," the president concluded. "See? She's smart. She's smart. She picked a Major League ball player. You know what it is to get the major leagues…. You got to be in shape. You can't look like these guys out here. No, she's great. But did anybody say, especially on the pandemic, has anybody said it better than that? That was this morning on Fox, *Fox & Friends*."

Filled with joy and completely humbled, Sean and I walked off the stage together. This was an incredibly special moment to me, and one I will never forget. I left the stage and went to the tent behind the stands. I changed Blake's diaper quickly, and soon after, the rally concluded. I hugged my family and rushed into the motorcade to head to our next stop.

As we rolled away in the motorcade, we passed the 7-Eleven that I used to go to in high school. I would leave my all-girls Catholic school, the Academy of the Holy Names, and head to the all-boys Catholic school, Jesuit High School, for cheerleading practice. Carpooling with a few other cheerleaders, we would always stop at the 7-Eleven, where I would grab a half Coke, half cherry Slurpee and Laffy Taffy. I loved the sparkle cherry bar with glass-like pieces of candy woven throughout. Now, I passed this same 7-Eleven in a presidential motorcade. I could hardly believe it.

⚉

I BOARDED AIR FORCE ONE after that Tampa rally, recharged and ready for the final two days of campaigning that lay ahead. On the way back to DC, we were supposed to stop in Fayetteville for a rally, but that was canceled due to weather. Our trip to Fort Bragg to visit our troops, however, was still a go. As we stopped for that final leg of the journey, I had no idea what I was in for. We approached Fort Bragg, the headquarters for the United States Army Special Operations Command, and we were all asked to turn off our phones. This was one of the biggest military installations in the world, and I was about to see it firsthand.

We arrived at the base, and President Trump spoke to several high-level base personnel before proceeding to speak to our troops. I walked in and watched his casual back and forth with our nation's heroes. He was so personable and conversational as he interacted with them and took their questions. Near the end of his remarks, he said, "You all know Kayleigh, right?" pointing to me at the back of the room. "Her husband is an MLB pitcher. He lost to the Dodgers, and he didn't look too happy today," he laughed.

After the president spoke, I got to speak to several of these servicemen in the elite Special Forces. One guy said, "It's cool to have you guys here. We see you all on TV." Another guy asked me for a picture and said he loved my briefings. And another said, "I would never want your job. It's tough."

"Sir, you have the tough job," I said, "Not me. It is an incredible honor to meet you."

Whether an MLB pitcher or a White House press secretary, nothing could compare to the unfettered bravery of these men and women.

"I think of you all when I'm riding on the Osprey. I realize this is the same aircraft you guys are on before landing to fight for us. Do you get nervous?" I asked.

"No," he said. "We want the green light from the president. We are ready for it, and we want that green light."

"*That's amazing,*" I thought. I could not imagine waiting for the green light to go into a perilous situation, much less wanting it. Meeting these heroes at Fort Bragg was undoubtedly one of the highlights of my time in the White House.

Not only was their bravery unfathomable but so, too, was their sacrifice. While I dreaded leaving my daughter for a few weeks or days, our servicemen and women left their families sometimes for months on end and not knowing if they would even return.

My time in the White House gave me what I needed—perspective. I remember one morning in June, I said goodbye to Blake as I left my DC apartment. I knew that my sister would be flying home with her, so this was goodbye—for a while. I brought Blake to Ryann, who was still sleeping that morning when I left. They cuddled up in bed, and I gave Blake a hug. I started to cry as I walked out the door and down the hall.

I went out the back car garage and into my "Carpet" vehicle. Carpet is a fleet of vehicles used by the executive branch. Operated by the White House Military Office, non-commissioned officers of the United States Army are tasked with driving these vehicles, providing home-to-work transportation services for key White House employees. Given my high visibility, the chief of staff allowed me to use this service.

During my rides, I met some incredible men and women in the United States Army, including one sergeant in particular whom I developed a friendship with. For purposes of this book, we will call him "Sergeant P." I knew I liked Sergeant P. right off the bat when one of our first rides developed into a back and forth about pizza. Dismissing the beloved New York City pizza, we debated which fast food pizza we loved most—Domino's? Pizza Hut? Or did the frozen Totino's pizza with small, cubed pepperonis eclipse them all?

That June morning when I got in the vehicle, I was not my typical, lighthearted self, having just left Blake behind. During the ride, Sergeant P. randomly said to me that he had been away from his daughter, and it's been hard.

"Are you okay?" he asked. "I hear you tearing up."

"I'm okay," I said through my tears. "I completely understand. I just left my daughter in my apartment, and she's about to fly home."

Sergeant P. then began to tell me that he had been away from his daughter for an entire year. Yes, a YEAR! His wife and his daughter lived in another state, and the Department of Defense had restricted travel within a certain number of miles due to COVID-19. This meant that he had to stay in DC.

"I missed her taking her first steps," he said.

Wow. My problems were nothing compared to Sergeant P.'s. I realized in that moment just how blessed I truly was.

"Not everyone understands," he said. "I want to take her to Disney, but I want her to be old enough to remember."

That drive with Sergeant P. made me eternally grateful for my time with my daughter. Our servicemen and women, whether driving an executive vehicle or participating in a Special Forces mission overseas, were the ones making the true sacrifice—a sacrifice I will never personally know but will always appreciate.

CHAPTER 13

A PARALLEL JOURNEY

"Each is the stroke of a brush on His beautiful canvas.
Each is the light of one star helping to form a galaxy..."

—Melissa in *I Still Believe*

As hard as it was to take those first steps to the podium, I knew that I had already been through a much harder battle—my battle with the breast cancer gene. I grew up knowing that my family had a history of breast cancer. Eight women in my family—mostly aunts and cousins on my mom's side—had been plagued with this horrible illness. Some were even in their young twenties.

During my senior year at Georgetown, a doctor suggested that my mom test for the BRCA gene. "Based on your family history, I can almost assure you that you have a genetic mutation," the doctor told her. She was right. My mom tested positive for the BRCA2 genetic mutation, putting her at a roughly 84 percent chance of breast cancer and a 27 percent chance of ovarian cancer.[1]

Though my mom did not have breast cancer, she had an extraordinarily high chance of getting it. She knew exactly what she wanted to do. Despite the concerns of some in my family, she decided to get a preventative double mastectomy. At the time, the measure seemed radical to many. Her surgery came before Angelina Jolie had shared that she carried a similar genetic mutation, opting to get the same procedure as my mother.

When my mom decided to remove her breast tissue in 2009, outside of the medical community, few understood her decision. But I did. I understood it all too well when I showed up in her hospital room and saw her lying there. As I described previously, "She looked gaunt and frail, but her physical appearance belied her internal strength."[2] My mom's decision to have this surgery brought her chances of breast cancer close to zero.

I knew that day, at the age of twenty-one, that I, too, wanted to test for the BRCA mutation. I had a fifty-fifty chance of having the gene, and knowledge was power. I took the test, and far sooner than I expected, I received a call from my doctor. Early one morning, close to Christmas, an unknown number appeared on my cell phone. Typically, I wouldn't answer a call like this, but I did this time.

"You've tested positive for the BRCA2 genetic mutation," my doctor told me.

Tears began to pour down my cheeks as I walked downstairs to share my diagnosis with my family. My dad was in the kitchen. He hugged me and said those powerful words I will never forget: "Kayleigh, you know your weakness. We all have one in life, but you know yours. You know your weakness, and you can attack it head on."

He was exactly right.

Initially, I set out to get the same surgery as my mom. I wanted to do it fairly quickly. Within the year, I had hoped. But I was single at the time. I wasn't sure what dating post-mastectomy would be like, and the unknown worried me. Knowing that my risk of breast cancer and ovarian cancer really did not start to rise until the age of thirty, instead of surgery, I resolved to engage in routine surveillance.

Every six months, I would go to Moffitt Cancer Center and receive either a mammogram or an MRI. Mammograms were often followed by an ultrasound since it was hard to see through my dense breast tissue. When I went to these appointments, I crossed paths with incredibly courageous women fighting this ugly disease. Some were in wheelchairs. Some had head scarfs, covering their bare scalps where locks of hair once lay. These women were heroes.

My nearly ten years of surveillance was nothing compared to what these women went through. As I wrote before, "My twenties have been a blessed decade, free from the ravages of cancer, but not the prospect of it."[3] Indeed, I had many scares and false alarms. Like the time in law school where all I wanted to do was study, but I just couldn't get the large, hard mass I found in my breast out of my mind. I was in Miami and away from my oncologist. The OBGYN in the area sent me to get a mammogram. Fortunately, it was nothing to worry about.

Or the time I had my first mammogram. I had just been through the rather awkward process—an experience every woman knows well. I was back in the waiting room with my mom when I met a lady who had battled cancer. "You don't have to worry unless they call you back for an ultrasound," she said. Sure enough, they did just that. "Kayleigh, we need to do an ultrasound," the nurse said. During the lonely walk back to the ultrasound, my mind was filled with fear as I lay down in the dark room. Certain I had cancer, tears gushed out as the nurse moved her wand across my breast. I would later learn that ultrasounds were going to be commonplace for me since my tissue was so dense. At the time, I did not know this.

After finishing undergrad, I entered the workforce, went to law school, and began dating. Breast cancer was a constant worry. But that all changed on May 1, 2018. On that day, nearly ten years after my diagnosis, I decided to have the same surgery as my mom. A big reason I had the confidence to make this decision was because I had found a supportive husband in Sean Gilmartin. We had been married six months earlier. He knew my plans to have a preventative double mastectomy, and he could not have been more reassuring, promising me that he would love me no matter what.

The night before my surgery, my family and I went to the Tampa Bay Lightning hockey game. My surgery required no food after midnight, and the Lightning game always offered an array of food—pizza, ice-cream, chicken fingers—you name it. But as I tried to enjoy the game (and the food), I was distracted by the burden on the horizon. That evening, I went home and spent some time writing my thoughts and praying, late into the evening.

The next morning, I took a shower and tried to take in the feeling of the hot water pouring over my breasts. My doctors had explained to me that, while my nipple-sparing mastectomy would leave me looking virtually unchanged, I would no longer be able to feel in that region. I tried to relish that last shower, sanitizing my body with the Hibiclens rinse that the doctor had given me. After my shower, I put on the pink hoodie and gray sweatpants that my mom had picked out for me, wanting her daughter to be as comfortable as possible. Then, I put on my gray socks, dotted with bright yellow lemons.

The lemon socks reminded me of a television series I was watching called *This Is Us*. In one scene, a new father had just lost one of his triplets at birth, and an older doctor with a soothing voice offered him this wisdom: "I like to think that one day you'll be an old man like me talking a young man's ear off explaining to him how you took the sourest lemon that life has to offer and turned it into something resembling lemonade."[4]

I smiled when I looked at those lemon socks. That's exactly what I was doing—turning lemons into lemonade. But I could not do it alone. The support of my husband and family and the strength of Jesus Christ were my rock. A day prior to my surgery, while flying home to Florida, I gazed out the window and down to earth when the lyrics of "Carry Me Through" played, reminding me that I would be climbing the mountain before me with the strength of Jesus Christ replacing my own.[5]

As it turns out, that is just what my Savior did. He carried me through with His strength. He also gave me a peace—that same peace I found when I went from tears in my West Wing office to total and complete serenity at the podium. Despite my apprehensions in the night leading up to my surgery, I had a strange calm in the pre-operation bed before being wheeled back to surgery. My only tears came when my dad huddled us all together to say a prayer. As he did, his voice became shaky, and he began to tear up. I had never seen him cry.

After the six-hour surgery, I woke up and saw my mom. My first words were: "That was easier than a CNN panel!" We still laugh at that. When they unveiled my dressings to reveal my breasts, I proclaimed with amazement, "Did they even do the surgery?!" The nipple-sparing procedure and implants in place left me looking almost the same. I still looked like me. More importantly than that, like my mom, I could now say with confidence that I would never die of breast cancer.

As I wrote previously, I now live life "free of fear and full of hope."[6] Even so, another scare—perhaps the scariest of all—was still on the horizon.

My husband and my Savior were instrumental in providing me with the confidence to take the step of having a preventative double mastectomy. But, as I wrote before, I credit those who came before me: "I'd like to think I'm strong, but my strength is enveloped in fear, a fear that is assuaged by women who have made this same decision. Women like Angelina Jolie, who wrote about her decision to have a preventative mastectomy. And women like my mother, who boldly took this step without hesitation. Their strength has become my own. It was important for me to share this with you for a very simple reason: this day was only made possible because of these women who so openly and publicly shared their experiences."[7]

In August of 2020, the Republican National Convention was approaching. I knew this would have tremendous viewership and provide an opportunity for me to share my BRCA journey on a national stage. It could help so many women. At the time, I was White House press secretary, and I called Jared Kushner one Saturday afternoon. "Jared, I think women should hear this story," I told him. He was in total agreement and made it happen.

I spent a lot of time on my speech. It would be short, and I wanted every single word to count. It needed to be 100 percent perfect. As my Wednesday night speech approached, I grew nervous. I would be sharing a highly personal story on a national stage. But just as Angelina Jolie sharing her decision gave me so much confidence, I knew I could do the same for other women.

That morning, as I got ready to go record my speech, President Trump called me before coming down to the Oval Office. President Trump compassionately said to me, "Everyone is excited about your speech. Deliver it emotionally and powerfully. This message is important."

We continued to talk, and I shared with him a little about my mastectomy, how far reconstruction has advanced, and how I had eliminated my chances of breast cancer. His call gave me so much courage, and it meant the world that he would think to call me ahead of this important moment. President Trump will never know just how much that call meant.

From the stage of the Republican National Convention, to an audience of 17.3 million viewers, I shared my story—my family history, my decision to get a mastectomy, and the aftermath.

"I was scared. The night before, I fought back tears as I prepared to lose a piece of myself," I shared. "But the next day, with my mom, dad, husband, and Jesus Christ by my side, I underwent a mastectomy, almost eliminating my chance of breast cancer— a decision I now celebrate."[8]

I also revealed some of my first calls following my surgery: "During one of my most difficult times, I expected to have the support of my family, but I had more support than I knew. As I came out of anesthesia, one of the first calls I received was from Ivanka Trump. Days later, as I recovered, my phone rang. It was President Trump, calling to check on me. I was blown away. Here was the leader of the free world caring about me."[9] The president's call came long before I worked for his campaign or in the White House. He was truly calling because he cared.

To this day, I still have women come up to me and say how much that speech meant to them. Some with breast cancer. Some have genetic mutations. Every story is unique. One in eight women will be diagnosed with breast cancer in their lifetime.[10] As women, we fight this fight together.

THE DAY AFTER MY speech, Chief of Staff Mark Meadows came into my office. It was a brief visit, and he had a simple message to convey: "Thank you for sharing about Jesus Christ last night. You said his name to millions of people."

I said the name "Jesus Christ" and will continue to proclaim the name of Jesus Christ because that is who I turn to in times of trouble. He always shows up.

I've recounted many of my BRCA scares previously, but this one I have not shared until now. While I am free of the fear of breast cancer, the BRCA2 genetic mutation also puts me at a 27 percent chance of ovarian cancer. My mom had completed her family when she chose to have a hysterectomy. As a BRCA2 carrier, though this procedure was an option, my doctor advised me that I could wait until the age of forty-five.

While my risk of ovarian cancer is lower than breast cancer, it is in some ways more of a worry because it is harder to detect. At my routine OBGYN yearly checkup, my doctor suggested I get a trans-vaginal ultrasound. After the test, she came to me with a disturbing finding. "You have a very suspicious mass on one of your ovaries," she informed me. "It looks to be vascular, meaning it has blood flow. You need to bring the results to Moffitt Cancer Center. They may need to remove your ovary."

I left the doctor that day in sheer panic. If they needed to remove both my ovaries, this would mean that I would not be able to have biological children unless the doctors were able to harvest my eggs. As newlyweds, Sean and I had a strong desire to have children. God had laid adoption on my heart at a very young age, and I wondered if maybe this was His plan for my life.

We met with my doctor at Moffitt Cancer Center, and he said that there would need to be further testing. The next step would be getting an MRI, and the results could determine if surgery would be needed. In a best-case scenario, the ultrasound would just be a false alarm. If the cyst presented the same troubling characteristics on an MRI that it did on an ultrasound, removing one or possibly even both of my ovaries could be necessary.

My husband and I went to Moffitt a few days later for an evening MRI. I went back to the MRI machine and lay on the table before being pulled back into the magnetic resonance imaging device. With a circular tube surrounding my body, I tried to listen closely to the music playing in the headphones that the technician had provided to me. It was difficult to focus with the loud clicks and bangs piercing my ears, as the machine's coils produced a magnetic field to generate imaging of my ovaries. Through the sharp, intrusive noises, I prayed to Jesus that this would just be a scare, and if it were in His will, that He would bless Sean and me with children.

He answered my prayer.

Shortly after the MRI, I learned that while the ultrasound had made the cyst look suspicious, it was in fact just a corpus luteum—a benign mass of cells that releases a hormone important to pregnancy. I cannot describe the relief I had and the freedom I felt upon learning the news. The scare set in motion our plans to have a child, and just over a year later, Baby Blake arrived.

And less than a year after that, He sent me to the White House, where I would spend one of my final days there dancing with Baby Blake during the White House Christmas party. With my one-year-old daughter in my arms, we danced as the Marine band played her favorite song—"Let it Go" from the movie *Frozen*. Afterward, she crawled around my office in her beautiful white dress as my whole family and I took in the moment.

My beautiful dance with Baby Blake in the White House came after navigating through a lot of worry, not just my health worry but also following my anxieties about taking my job in the White House. Before leaving Florida to become White House press secretary, I expressed to Sean my fears of leaving Blake and my apprehensions in starting my new role at such a tough time in American history. "I want you to see something," he said, insisting that I sit down and watch a movie with him. He put on a film that I had never seen called *I Still Believe*, which told the story of Christian musician Jeremy Camp.[11] I had heard Jeremy's music before but never knew the backstory.

While in college and pursuing a career in music, Jeremy Camp fell in love with a fellow student named Melissa. The beautiful blonde-haired, blue-eyed girl—as depicted in the film—was unfortunately diagnosed with liver cancer. Instead of running from the unimaginable situation, Jeremy proposed to Melissa. Melissa's cancer moved from her liver to her ovaries, and the doctors told her that they would need to remove her ovaries. But, in a miraculous turn of events, the doctors call off the surgery, and Melissa is pronounced cancer-free. Jeremy and Melissa got married, but unfortunately the cancer returned, taking Melissa from Jeremy far too soon at the young age of twenty-one. Jeremy begins to question God and has quite a tumultuous internal battle. In an incredible ending scene that I will never forget, Jeremy smashes his guitar to find a note from Melissa she had hidden before she passed.

"Jeremy, I know you'll find this someday. See, I'm finally letting you read my journal," the note from Melissa read. "You're asleep on my shoulder right now. I guess one of the benefits of the pain is it's hard to sleep, which means I have a lot of time to think. And I've thought a lot about the stories you like to tell at your concert.... Ancient stories, still relevant and true. In one story, God grants healing. Miracles do happen. Yet, to another, his call is to suffer and even die. And I realized something, they both have value because each is a chapter in a bigger story. Each is the stroke of a brush on His beautiful canvas. Each is the light of one star helping to form a galaxy, and I think I'm one of those lucky people meant to experience both…I've learned that suffering doesn't destroy faith, it refines it. And God is worth trusting, even when you can't see.… So do one thing for me, Jeremy Camp.… When you're ready, pick up your guitar."[12]

These words transform Jeremy's life and restore his faith, leading him to indeed pick up his guitar and author those famous lyrics I grew up listening to. The movie concludes with Jeremy Camp standing on a stage and singing those moving lyrics with all of the conviction in the world. Jeremy chose to leave his doubt, his confusion, his hurt in the past and instead proclaim those remarkable three words while strumming his guitar in front of a crowd of thousands: "I still believe." Even though he could not see, as he sang, "I still believe."[13]

I cried as I watched that final scene of *I Still Believe*. Despite unimaginable pain and suffering after losing his young bride, Jeremy could proclaim, "I still believe." For some reason, totally unbeknownst to me, my scare with an ovarian ultrasound turned out much different than Melissa's. God decided to keep me here on earth, as I gave birth to Blake and took on a new role in DC. Melissa, on the other hand, left her earthly home far too soon, but this amazing woman of faith had realized an incredible truth: "[E]ach is a chapter in a bigger story.… Each is the light of one star helping to form a galaxy.…"

And that galaxy extends far beyond our time here on earth. As I move forward in life, I do not know what the future holds. I hope to have more children. Who knows where my career path in media and politics will lead me? I hope to stay healthy and have a nice life with Sean, Blake, and our future children. But these are all hopes, and life brings uncertainties. No matter what lies ahead in my journey through life, I do know of one certainty: Jesus Christ will be there through every hurdle and hardship. He will carry me through life's valleys, celebrate with me through life's peaks.

Just as He guided my path to the podium and to my husband, He will guide me through the future—taking me to places I don't yet know, putting me in a certain time, in a certain place, in a certain life circumstance for a reason. You see, Christ put me in this BRCA gene body for a purpose. He guided my path to Washington and put a love for politics in my heart at a young age for a purpose.

The same goes for you.

We are all a small piece of a much bigger puzzle. The Savior that I know will guide you through life if you just let Him. This was something I learned early on. I remember going to a bookstore in Plant City, Florida, with my mom when I just a young girl. I was immediately attracted to a bookmark on display. It depicted a beach with one set of footprints along the sand. It had a blue tassel, and the words on the bookmark recounted a famous story called "Footprints in the Sand."

As the famous story goes, a man had a dream one night about traversing a sandy beach with the Lord. As he walked, visions of life flashed across the night sky. He noticed that along the sand, there were not always two sets of footprints—one belonging to him and one belonging to Christ. At times, he saw just one set of footprints, especially during the hardest times in life. The man questioned why the Lord would abandon him at his lowest times. As the wise story goes, "The Lord replied, 'My precious, precious child, I love you and I would never leave you. During your times of trial and suffering, when you see only one set of footprints…it was then that I carried you.'"[14]

That is a truth I know all too well.

God has for you a plan, a purpose. No one can stop His plan for your life. He will lead you to victory and carry you through the trials if you only let Him. What my dad told me in the wake of my fears is true for you as well.

Indeed, you are here "for such a time as this."

This is my story. But, rest assured, He has already written yours.

ACKNOWLEDGMENTS

Baby Blake—Your sweet smile has brought joy to so many hearts. You changed my life forever and filled me with a love that I had never experienced. As I wrote this book, I had you in my mind, sweet baby girl. You are truly the most beautiful chapter of my life story.

Sean—You are the love of my life, my rock, and the quiet strength I turn to through life's valleys. You have held my hand through every step of this exciting journey. You are my soulmate and will have my heart forever.

Dad, Mike McEnany—You are the faith leader of our family. Together, you and mom have engrained in me a love for Jesus Christ. You are an inspiring leader, a man of great character, and someone I look to for wisdom. I know that I am biased, but God truly blessed me with the greatest father in the world.

Mom, Leanne McEnany—I can say without hesitation that I would have never achieved my dreams if not for you. We had so many late nights in our kitchen, talking about the hurdles I faced either in dating or in my career. You traveled the country with me, making sure that Baby Blake always saw her mommy, no matter how many strollers needed to be broken down or Pack 'n Plays loaded onto airplanes. You gave your whole self to your children, and for that, I am eternally grateful.

My brother, Michael—I am always so proud when I share with the world that my brother is a doctor in emergency medicine. Along with your bright mind, you have a heart of gold. When America shut down during COVID-19, you worked on the front lines. Thank you.

My sister, Ryann—You are beautiful, smart, and the kindest young woman I know. You lived this journey right alongside me. I cherish those moments on the campaign trail when I landed on Air Force One and walked across the tarmac to the rally to find my beautiful, smiling sister interviewing the amazing Trump rally-goers. Though I might have been annoyed at your midnight cooking ventures in our small DC apartment when I was pregnant, I will always hold those days close to my heart.

Paul and JoAnna Gilmartin—You are the best in-laws any spouse could hope for. Paul, you are a self-described "common-sense American." Your political insight and ideas keep me thoroughly engaged. JoAnna, your motherly instincts have been invaluable in helping with Baby Blake. You both have raised the perfect man for me.

Michael Gilmartin—As my brother-in-law, you have been an invaluable piece of the puzzle. You have always been there to support our family and the cause.

Chad Gilmartin—Words cannot adequately describe the important role you have played in my personal life and professional career. I'll never forget meeting Sean and hearing about his brilliant and politically inclined cousin. You have an incredible mind, a burning passion, and the fight within you. My press briefings would not have been possible if not for you. You were the key to making it all come together. Thank you for being an exceptional colleague, a sounding board, and a friend. You have a bright future ahead.

Mema—As I write these words, it is your birthday: July 21, 2021. We mourn the first birthday without you here on earth, but I know Heaven is celebrating your very first birthday with Christ. I will never forget our long nights of red wine and pizza during law school. You were always the life of the party, and I can't wait to see you again!

Poppy—We lost you far too soon. Your generally quiet demeanor was always punctuated by a fantastic sense of humor. You had common sense, wisdom, and—most of all—a beautiful heart. See you soon!

Nana—You have been by my side through Georgetown, Oxford, Harvard, and beyond. You, my mom, and I have had so many fun trips together and incredible memories. Thank you for being a wonderful grandmother and always supporting my career path. Most of all, thank you for being a great woman of faith in our family.

Aunt Linda and Uncle Smoke—You are two of the greatest supporters of President Trump and have been there every step of the way cheering on my career. I love you both and thank you for representing the McEnanys well!

Aunt Andie and Uncle George—Coming to visit you in the Florida Keys during mini lobster season has become a family tradition! I have a blast every time I'm with you both. You radiate happiness and joy and always keep me laughing. Love you!

Will, Nicki, Uncle Bill, Aunt Donna, and William—I love you all and thank you for all of your support! I cherish our Christmases together and think so highly of each and every one of you!

Suzanne Scott—When I was just an intern at Fox News, you took the time to meet with me. I was a college student, and you were an executive, but you cared enough to give a young woman encouragement. You gave me the advice and the courage to pursue my dreams, and I am honored to now call you my boss.

Sean Hannity—I went from intern to a weekly guest on your show, and you were instrumental in making that happen. Your courage, confidence, and fight shaped me along my journey. You have left your mark on the conservative movement.

Alan Colmes—Before I even became an intern on *Hannity & Colmes*, you took the time to acknowledge me in the greenroom. When I was at CNN, you sent me great advice on how to stay calm in those heated moments. I miss you, and I thank you for your mentorship.

Governor Mike Huckabee—God knew what He was doing when He placed me with your show for the first three years of my career. You are an absolutely brilliant communicator and a wonderful person. Also, in case no one told you, you have raised a pretty incredible daughter.

Sarah Huckabee Sanders—We crossed paths in the greenroom long before you or I became White House press secretary. You set an amazing example for me, and I followed in your footsteps in reading *Jesus Calling* before every press briefing.

Harris Faulkner—You are one of the best journalists out there, and you have a beautiful soul. I was so honored to join you on the airwaves during my time at the Republican National Committee, the Trump campaign, and the White House. Sitting next to you on the *Outnumbered* couch every day is truly humbling.

Emily Compagno—You radiate beauty and kindness. One of the greatest parts of my new role at Fox News was meeting you. You are our "legal eagle" and, more importantly, a friend. I look forward to what our future holds!

Julia Hahn—"Wow" is the only word I have to describe you. When I started as press secretary in the final year of the Trump administration, you had been there from the very beginning. Immediately, I recognized your talent and intelligence, and I can say emphatically that you were the "standout" member of the administration that I met during my tenure. Always able to identify the one angle of an argument no one had conceived, you have a bright future, and I will always be your biggest fan!

Lyndee Rose—When people inquire about "my binder," you immediately come to mind. The organization of my binder had nothing to do with me and everything to do with you. You were my executive assistant during the White House, but that title hardly describes your meaning to my life. Far more important than my binder, you have become a part of my family. You were by my side every step of the way at the White House, and you are forever a part of my future.

Judd Deere—The White House press shop could not have functioned without you. You kept the wheels in motion, ensuring every reporter had an answer to their inquiry and making sure all logistics were perfectly in place. You bestowed upon me all the institutional knowledge I needed upon coming into the White House. You were, without a doubt, a true leader on the press team.

Brian Morgenstern—You joined the press shop as we were in the thick of many battles. You were a wonderful and important contribution to the team, and you rose to the occasion often. You were unafraid to battle on liberal media networks and showed true fight and grit.

Margo Martin—You are smart, tough, and as kind as they come. You did such a wonderful job on behalf of President Trump and your country, and I am blessed to have worked with you!

Karoline Leavitt, Harrison Fields, and Jalen Drummond—Every time I type your names or find a text from one of you on my phone, a smile comes to my face. You three were my lights in the White House when the going got tough. No matter the day, I could count on your positivity. Your intellect and work ethic goes without saying!

Gaby Hurt and Davis Ingle—You two kept the press in line and operated with true professionalism. Each one of you has a bright future, and I am so thankful for the dedication and long hours that you put into the job!

John McEntee—You played a key role in my transition to the White House. You always had faith in my ability to take the podium, and I so appreciate your advocacy and friendship! Beyond that, you always encouraged the president to stay true to the promises he made to the MAGA movement!

Stephen Miller, Derek Lyons, Robert O'Brien, Dan Scavino, Tony Ornato, Brooke Rollins, Avi Berkowitz—You all made the job so much easier. You are true professionals, intellects, and superior in each of your fields.

Nick Luna, Cassidy Dumbauld, and Molly Michael—You each contributed so much to the administration. As steady and solid anchors, you laid the foundation for so much good.

Scott Atlas—When everyone was wrong, you were right. You came into my office and you laid out the science in support of children in schools and against onerous lockdowns that harmed innocent Americans. History should look upon you fondly.

Chad Wolf, Alex Azar, Robert Redfield, and so many more—You were not just cabinet secretaries and heads of agencies, but purveyors of accurate information to the American People.

Mark Meadows—You were a constant reminder of faith and Jesus Christ during my time in the White House. Always prioritizing faith and family, you knew what was most important in life. Thank you for being an inspiring leader for the entire West Wing.

Jared Kushner and Ivanka Trump—Long before I was ever in the White House, you made time for me. In addition to giving me advice and encouragement, you always had your eye on how you could make substantive changes that would better the lives of the American People. From Middle East peace deals and criminal justice reform to paid family leave for federal workers and the Women's Global Development and Prosperity Fund, you both have changed lives.

Lara Trump—You radiate joy and our shared Christian faith shines within you. You were instrumental in my move from media to politics, and I am forever grateful for your faith in me. You are an example to women everywhere.

Eric and Don Trump Jr.—You both have been so kind to me during my time in politics. Eric, I loved crossing paths with you in greenrooms through New York City. Don, I will never forget the time that you voluntarily held Baby Blake during our flight back from the Iowa caucuses!

Tim Murtaugh—You have the quickest wit of anyone I know. You are sharp, loyal, and—most important of all—kind. I was so blessed to have you as my communications director during my time on the Trump campaign.

Anthony Ziccardi—You had faith in this book from the VERY beginning. You believed in me from the get-go, and I am so very grateful that you brought me on to the Post Hill Press team. I will always appreciate your faith, encouragement, and engagement through this process!

Kelsey Merritt—You are truly wonderful. The dedication, time, and passion you have put into helping promote this book has been unparalleled. You are smart, dedicated, and kind, and I cherished my time working with you.

Madeline Sturgeon, Rachel Hoge, and Holly Layman—You have facilitated the editing of this book and have both done a superb job in making sure this manuscript is the best it could possibly be. Thank you!

Cody Corcoran—You designed the perfect cover for this book. We went through many iterations and changes, and you were meticulous, innovative, and patient until we agreed upon the perfect art for this project!

Bryan Manicchia—I have gone to your studio, Studio Artistry, since I was a cheerleader at Jesuit High School. You have taken my headshots from high school to CNN and beyond. When it came to taking a cover shot for the book, there was only one place I wanted to go: Studio Artistry!

Shealah Craighead, Joyce Boghosian, Tia Dufour, Randy Florendo, and Andrea Hanks—You captured every historic moment of our time in the Trump White House. Your pictures captured the essence of the Trump administration, and it was a true pleasure to get to know each one of you.

David Limbaugh—We met about a year before this book went to print, and you quickly became one of my favorite people. You are a relentless advocate for conservatism, an incredible writer and commentator, and—most importantly—a brother in Christ whose kind spirit shines through.

Rush Limbaugh—I listened to you my entire life. *The Rush Limbaugh Show* played each day in my father's truck, and I took in every moment. You are, without a doubt, the reason I pursued a career in politics. Your legacy continues through the countless young men and women you inspired.

Vice President Pence—You were a true Christian light in the White House. From signaling prayer hands in my direction before my briefing and reciting Christian lyrics in the hallways of the West Wing, you are a true man of God and a great leader.

President Trump—You gave me the opportunity and the honor of a lifetime when you appointed me to be the 33rd White House press secretary. Early on in the 2016 presidential campaign, I recognized your boldness in standing strong against political correctness and for conservatism. Your administration courageously stood for faith, conservatism, and freedom. Well done.

Jesus Christ—Many times through my life, there was one set of footprints. In those moments, you were carrying me through trialss and tribulations. Nothing in life is certain with one exception: YOU. Thank you for sacrificing your life for humanity. You are the way, the truth, and the life.

ENDNOTES

Chapter 1

1 *Trump says 'justice will be served' as federal authorities investigate George Floyd's death*, Fox9, May 27, 2020 (https://tinyurl.com/s23vw8aa).

2 Janell Ross, *'That's not going to bring my brother back': George Floyd's brother calls for end to violence*, NBC News, June 1, 2020 (https://tinyurl.com/334rvnym).

3 Bill Hutchinson, *'We're sick of it': Protesters explain method to the madness of violent demonstrations*, ABC News, May 31, 2020 (https://tinyurl.com/4knxa5wp).

4 Gloria Gomez & FOX 13 staff, *New video shows Tampa looters shattering gas station's doors as smoke pours from Champs Sports*, FOX 13, June 1, 2020 (https://tinyurl.com/ma369762).

5 *Ibid.*

6 Peter Baker, *In Days of Discord, a President Fans the Flames*, New York Times, May 30, 2020 (https://tinyurl.com/4cc4ssn7).

7 "Remarks by President Trump at Kennedy Space Center," The White House, May 30, 2020 (https://tinyurl.com/v7wukrkr).

8 Stacy Liberatore, *NASA-SpaceX Falcon 9 rocket launch has just a 50 percent chance of liftoff for Saturday and could be moved to Sunday if weather does not improve*, Daily Mail, May 29, 2020 (https://tinyurl.com/5xfr8ej2).

9 "Donald Trump Speech Transcript at Kennedy Space Center After SpaceX NASA Launch," Rev.com, May 30, 2020 (https://tinyurl.com/2ryamamm).

10 "Remarks by President Trump at Kennedy Space Center," The White House.

11 Emma Tucker, *Trump Was Whisked Away to an Underground Bunker During White House Protests: NYT*, Daily Beast, May 31, 2020 (https://tinyurl.com/mw84b5jv).

12 John Cassidy, *A Night of Violent Protests Sets a Nation Ablaze*, The New Yorker, May 30, 2020 (https://tinyurl.com/w83wy3zt).

13 Elizabeth Landers, Twitter, May 31, 2020 (https://tinyurl.com/ufffhn7z).

14 Mayor Muriel Bowser, Twitter, May 31, 2020 (https://tinyurl.com/7rjpeyh3).

15 "King's World House," The Martin Luther King Jr. Research and Education Center, Stanford University (https://tinyurl.com/r6ad6nps).

16 "St. John's Church," The White House Historical Association, (https://tinyurl.com/7spkuwhk).

17 "History," Saint John's Church, (https://tinyurl.com/fhtc43tk).

18 "St. John's Church," The White House Historical Association, (https://tinyurl.com/7spkuwhk).

19 "The Hymnal," The Protestant Episcopal Church in the United States of America, October 1916: 454 (https://tinyurl.com/585ts3es).

20 *Ibid.*

21 "Press Briefing by Press Secretary Kayleigh McEnany," The White House, June 1, 2020 (https://tinyurl.com/23pzrm3b).

22 Crystal Bonvillian, *Retired police captain killed on Facebook Live while protecting friend's pawn shop*, KIRO 7, June, 3, 2020 (https://tinyurl.com/ks3tyjd7).

23 "Press Briefing by Press Secretary Kayleigh McEnany," The White House, June 3, 2020 (https://tinyurl.com/w3ajcw).

24 "Remarks by President Trump at Signing of an Executive Order on Safe Policing for Safe Communities," The White House, June 16, 2020 (https://tinyurl.com/83bwzn8).

25 Kayleigh McEnany, *The New American Revolution: The Making of a Populist Movement*, Simon & Schuster, January 9, 2018 (https://tinyurl.com/y3uyex5u).

Chapter 2

1 Megan Bomba, "Hard Work Beats Talent When Talent Doesn't Work Hard," Team USA, April 3, 2019 (https://tinyurl.com/387z99cc).

2 "Department of Justice Report Regarding the Criminal Investigation into the Shooting Death of Michael Brown by Ferguson, Missouri Police Officer Darren Wilson," The Department of Justice, March 4, 2015 (https://tinyurl.com/3fekht5f).

3 Adam Steinbaugh, "After Harvard Law School Reaffirms Commitment to Free Speech, a 'Little Sign War' Erupts," Foundation for Individual Rights in Education, April 1, 2016 (https://tinyurl.com/smerv4a).

4 Kayleigh McEnany, *The New American Revolution*.

5 *"READ: Amy Coney Barrett's Opening Statement In Her Confirmation Hearing*, October 11, 2020 (https://tinyurl.com/39v7zu32).

6 "What Is the Meaning of 'Iron Sharpens Iron' in Proverbs 27:17," Mel Walker, Christianity.com, September 5, 2019 (https://tinyurl.com/4d5yz9jv).

7 Kate Taylor, *'Guess that's 2020 for ya': Domino's responds to Twitter backlash over thanking a Trump staffer for a Compliment 8 Years Ago*, June 16, 2020 (https://tinyurl.com/2wd65669).

8 *Ibid.*
9 *Ibid.*

Chapter 3

1 Ken Moritsugu, "New Chinese virus cases decline, but tracking method revised again," PBS, February 20, 2020 (https://tinyurl.com/3p8wutsz).
2 *Ibid.*

Chapter 4

1 Devan Cole, "Fauci admits earlier Covid-19 mitigation efforts would have saved more American lives," CNN, April 12, 2020 (https://tinyurl.com/45ev57ap).
2 "Outbreak of Pneumonia of Unknown Etiology (PUE) in Wuhan, China," CDC, January 8, 2020 (https://tinyurl.com/btr5usf7).
3 "Update and Interim Guidance on Outbreak of 2019 Novel Coronavirus (2019-nCoV) in Wuhan, China," CDC, January 17, 2020 (https://tinyurl.com/3m9nnuc6).
4 "Public Health Screening to Begin at 3 U.S. Airports for 2019 Novel Coronavirus ('2019-nCoV')," CDC, January 17, 2020 (https://tinyurl.com/9dk84h3p).
5 "Transcript of Update on 2019 Novel Coronavirus (2019-nCoV)," CDC, January 21, 2020 (https://tinyurl.com/5f45zcpy).
6 "Proclamation on Suspension of Entry as Immigrants and Nonimmigrants of Persons who Post a Risk of Transmitting 2019 Novel Coronavirus," The White House, January 31, 2020 (https://tinyurl.com/8vcj5hu6).
7 Becket Adams, "Yes, Biden absolutely did oppose the China travel restrictions and call them 'xenophobic,'" *Washington Examiner*, October 8, 2020 (https://tinyurl.com/3yna7xd8).
8 Allison Aubrey, "Trump Declares Coronavirus A Public Health Emergency and Restricts Travel From China," NPR, January 31, 2020 (https://tinyurl.com/5ufed7nr); "Past epidemics prove fighting coronavirus with travel bans is a mistake," *Washington Post*, February 2, 2020 (https://tinyurl.com/7zzbm-bet); "Trump's travel ban expansion is an unexpected win – for China," *Washington Post*, February 1, 2020 (https://tinyurl.com/tuye7uzn); Gregg Re, "After attacking Trump's coronavirus-related China travel ban as xenophobic, Dems and media have changed tune," Fox News, April 1, 2020 (https://tinyurl.com/4dj2ykc2).
9 "Remarks by President Trump, Vice President Pence, and Members of the Coronavirus Task Force in Press Briefing," The White House, April 14, 2020 (https://tinyurl.com/c3jrnpuv).

10 "Inside the White House: Tour the West Wing," The White House (https://tinyurl.com/53ht3c5c).

11 "Trump Leaves White House Grounds for First Time Since March 28," *Reuters*, May 1, 2020 (https://tinyurl.com/yepf6774).

Chapter 5

1 "The Opposite of Courage Is Not Cowardice; It Is Conformity," Quote Investigator (https://tinyurl.com/bzzp8scy).

2 "Press Briefing by Press Secretary Kayleigh McEnany," The White House, May 6, 2020 (https://tinyurl.com/3eupkp7h).

3 Jayne O'Donnell, "Top disease official: Risk of coronavirus in USA is 'minuscule'; skip mask and wash hands," *USA Today*, updated February 19, 2020 (https://tinyurl.com/5sm94n75).

4 Lindsey Ellefson, "Vox Deletes January Tweet About Coronavirus That Really Has Not Aged Well," *Vox*, March 24, 2020 (https://tinyurl.com/mt84haha).

5 "Get a grippe, America. The flu is a much bigger threat than coronavirus, for now," *Washington Post*, February 1, 2020 (https://tinyurl.com/eawz6txc).

6 "How our brains make coronavirus seem scarier than it is," *Washington Post*, January 31, 2020 (https://tinyurl.com/dyskjf9p).

7 Megan Specia, Constant Méheut, and Christopher F. Schuetze, "In Europe, Fear Spreads Faster Than the Coronavirus Itself," *New York Times*, February 18, 2020 (https://tinyurl.com/kut2bwru).

8 Allison Aubrey, "Worried About Catching The New Coronavirus? In The U.S., Flu Is A Bigger Threat," NPR, January 29, 2020 (https://tinyurl.com/ysc2r2sd).

9 "Why we should be wary of an aggressive government response to coronavirus," *Washington Post*, February 3, 2020 (https://tinyurl.com/yvs7tpmh).

10 "Press Briefing by Press Secretary Kayleigh McEnany," The White House, May 6, 2020 (https://tinyurl.com/3eupkp7h).

11 Brian Flood, "Jen Psaki slammed for 'homophobic' tweet about Sen. Lindsey Graham," Fox News, February 3, 2021 (https://tinyurl.com/8w599b7v).

12 *Ibid.*

13 "Press Briefing by Press Secretary Jen Psaki, January 20, 2021," The White House, January 20, 2021 (https://tinyurl.com/ksc4rda8).

14 *Ibid.*

15 "Press Briefing by Press Secretary Jen Psaki and Deputy Director of the National Economic Council Bharat Ramamurti, March 9, 2021," The White House, March 9, 2021 (https://tinyurl.com/t9dytrup).

16 "Press Briefing by Press Secretary Jen Psaki, June 3, 2021," The White House, June 3, 2021 (https://tinyurl.com/wy7uyv8a).

17 "Press Briefing by Press Secretary Kayleigh McEnany," The White House, June 19, 2020 (https://tinyurl.com/7jv9a2bh).

18 "Press Briefing by Press Secretary Kayleigh McEnany," The White House, May 6, 2020 (https://tinyurl.com/3eupkp7h).

19 "Press Briefing by Press Secretary Kayleigh McEnany," The White House, June 29, 2020 (https://tinyurl.com/27au82ts).

20 "Does President Trump believe that it was a good thing that the South lost the Civil War?," YouTube, June 29, 2020 (https://tinyurl.com/2dj5f8jc).

21 "The Trump Campaign Is Seeking 'Hidden' Women Voters. Impeachment Won't Help," New York Times, October 31, 2019 (https://tinyurl.com/4em7km2t).

22 Kayleigh McEnany, Twitter, December 15, 2020 (https://tinyurl.com/vw4t96mj).

23 Maggie Haberman, Twitter, December 15, 2020 (https://tinyurl.com/ed4f8zay).

24 Thomas E. Patterson, "News Coverage of Donald Trump's First 100 Days," Harvard Kennedy School Shorenstein Center on Media, Politics and Public Policy, May 18, 2017 (https://tinyurl.com/2zhwcfbx).

25 Sara Fischer, "92% of Republicans think media intentionally reports fake news," Axios, June 27, 2018 (https://tinyurl.com/3kc6khf3).

26 Felix Salmon, "Media trust hits new low," Axios, January 21, 2021 (https://tinyurl.com/59zjh2wy).

27 Ibid.

28 Joe Concha, "US Just finished dead last among 46 countries in media trust – here's why," The Hill, June 28, 2021 (https://tinyurl.com/vfxv8534).

29 David Rutz, "Botched '60 Minutes' DeSantis story latest mainstream media hit piece on potential 2024 GOP contender," Fox News, April 6, 2021 (https://tinyurl.com/d4aewxb5).

30 Joseph A. Wulfsohn, "Washington Post runs 'fact-check' on Tim Scott's ancestry but not on Kamala Harris' 'Fweedom' plagiarism claim," Fox News, April 23, 2021 (https://tinyurl.com/ar9b26ch).

31 Maggie Haberman, "Kayleigh McEnany heckles the press. Is that all?" New York Times, August 3, 2020 (https://tinyurl.com/2hnphhrb).

32 Chris Cillizza, "Decoding the mysteries of Kayleigh McEnany's briefing book," CNN, July 17, 2020 (https://tinyurl.com/3jaw7bus).

33 Erik Wemple, "Kayleigh McEnany Watch: So Organized!," Washington Post, July 17, 2020 (https://tinyurl.com/4ahcvrcs).

34 Andrew Malcolm, "In Kayleigh McEnany, President Trump has finally found a skilled spokes-partner," McClatchy, July 28, 2020 (https://tinyurl.com/w9fe77u7).

35 "Press Briefing by Press Secretary Kayleigh McEnany," The White House, July 6, 2020 (https://tinyurl.com/y72uxrrk).

36 Press Briefing by Press Secretary Kayleigh McEnany | 7/16/2020," The White House, July 16, 2020 (https://tinyurl.com/ys8rfspa).

37 Joshua Rhett Miller, "'Hey, Karen': Chicago mayor Lori Lightfoot rips Kayleigh McEnany," *New York Post*, July 17, 2020 (https://tinyurl.com/6frpctb4).

38 *Ibid.*

39 "Attorney General William P. Barr Announces Results of Operation Legend," The Department of Justice, December 23, 2020 (https://tinyurl.com/m6xb664k).

40 "Remarks by President Trump in Press Briefing | August 13, 2020," The White House, August 13, 2020 (https://tinyurl.com/8t5tvj28).

Chapter 6

1 "Protesters Dispersed With Tear Gas So Trump Could Pose at Church," *New York Times,* June 1, 2020 (https://tinyurl.com/yk6tzs2p).

2 Peter Roff, "Who's Checking the Fact Checkers?" *U.S. News & World Report*, May 28, 2013 (https://tinyurl.com/zwruukds).

3 Tim Graham, "Tim Graham 'Fact-checkers' are pro-Biden, biased against Trump," Fox News, September 10, 2020 (https://tinyurl.com/wyk3ny8).

4 *Ibid.*

5 Edwin J. Feulner, Ph.D., "The Facts About Fact-Checkers," Heritage Foundation, July 11, 2018 (https://tinyurl.com/wxx6radt).

6 "Russia Secretary Offered Afghan Militants Bounties to Kill U.S. Troops, Intelligence Says," *New York Times*, June 26, 2020 (https://tinyurl.com/8jrce6rh).

7 Morgan Phillips, "Biden used Russian bounty story against Trump in 2020 campaign," Fox News, April 16, 2021 (https://tinyurl.com/zm2k3a37).

8 "Press Briefing by Press Secretary Kayleigh McEnany," The White House, June 29, 2020 (https://tinyurl.com/27au82ts).

9 Drew Holden, Twitter, April 15, 2021 (https://tinyurl.com/54v625x2).

10 Drew Holden, Twitter, April 15, 2021 (https://tinyurl.com/54v625x2).

11 Adam Rawnsley, Spencer Ackerman, and Asawin Suebsaeng, "US Intel Walks Back Claim Russians Put Bounties on American Troops," *Daily Beast*, April 15, 2021 (https://tinyurl.com/n93y5bh5).

12 David Rutz, "New York Times 'buried' bombshell that John Kerry told Iran about Israeli covert operations in Syria: Critics," Fox News, April 26, 2021 (https://tinyurl.com/eprazhpz).

13 "Press Briefing by Press Secretary Kayleigh McEnany," The White House, June 30, 2020 (https://tinyurl.com/5xj4djsh).

14 *Ibid.*

15 Morgan Chalfant, "Trump says he has seen evidence linking coronavirus to Wuhan lab," *The Hill*, April 30, 2020 (https://tinyurl.com/5yepzxz5).

16 Geoff Brumfiel, "Scientists Debunk Lab Accident Theory Of Pandemic Emergence," NPR, April 22, 2020 (https://tinyurl.com/b4tnvu).

17 "Senator Tom Cotton Repeats Fringe Theory of Coronavirus Origins," *New York Times*, February 17, 2020 (https://tinyurl.com/3hxje239).

18 "Was the new coronavirus accidentally released from a Wuhan lab? It's doubtful," *Washington Post*, May 1, 2020 (https://tinyurl.com/h5pzhjww).

19 Chris Cillizza, "Anthony Fauci just crushed Donald Trump's theory on the origins of the coronavirus," CNN, May 5, 2020 (https://tinyurl.com/jxms8z7r).

20 Kylie Atwood, "Pompeo-led effort to hunt down Covid lab theory shut down by Biden administration over concerns about quality of evidence," CNN, May 26, 2021 (https://tinyurl.com/vcu3nt4e).

21 Morgan Phillips, "Fauci 'not convinced' COVID-19 developed naturally," Fox News, May 23, 2021 (https://tinyurl.com/df8up3be).

22 "Timeline: How the Wuhan lab-leak theory suddenly became credible," *Washington Post*, May 25, 2021 (https://tinyurl.com/429urrzw).

23 Tom Gjelten, "Peaceful Protesters Tear-Gassed To Clear Way For Trump Church Photo-Op," *NPR*, June 1, 2020 (https://tinyurl.com/pbkk3ast).

24 "Inside the push to tear-gas protesters ahead of a Trump photo op," *Washington Post*, June 1, 2020 (https://tinyurl.com/cttpumfb).

25 "From Tiananmen Square to Lafayette Square," *Washington Post*, June 4, 2020 (https://tinyurl.com/ywbzusuh).

26 "Press Briefing by Press Secretary Kayleigh McEnany," The White House, June 3, 2020 (https://tinyurl.com/w3ajcw).

27 *Ibid.*

28 "Statement from Inspector General Mark Lee Greenblatt Regarding Special Review Report 'Review of U.S. Park Police Actions at Lafayette Park,'" Office of Inspector General U.S. Department of the Interior, June 9, 2021 (https://tinyurl.com/3k7mwx59).

29 Ken Dilanian, "Police did not clear D.C.'s Lafayette Square of protesters so Trump could hold a photo op, new report says," NBC News, June 9, 2021 (https://tinyurl.com/bu2mu8m7).

30 Kayla Rivas, "Fauci backs 'double-masking' in coronavirus fight, says 'likely more effective,'" Fox News, January 25, 2020 (https://tinyurl.com/becbxeep).

31 "Press Briefing by Press Secretary Kayleigh McEnany | 7/16/2020," The White House, July 16, 2020 (https://tinyurl.com/ys8rfspa).

32 Jim Acosta, Twitter, July 16, 2020 (https://tinyurl.com/42aps4p8).

33 Allan Smith, "White House press secretary: 'The science should not stand in the way of' schools fully reopening," NBC News, July 16, 2020 (https://tinyurl.com/srujb438).

34 Jessica Chasmar, "Jake Tapper scolds reporters for misconstruing Kayleigh McEnany's 'science' comments: 'Be fair,'" *Washington Times*, July 17, 2020 (https://tinyurl.com/uypw3psf).

35 Press Briefing by Press Secretary Kayleigh McEnany | 7/9/2020," The White House, July 9, 2020 (https://tinyurl.com/6cnhcdm7).

36 Emma-Jo Morris and Gabrielle Fonrouge, "Hunter Biden emails show leveraging connections with his father to boost Burisma pay," *New York Post*, October 14, 2020 (https://tinyurl.com/7arhwbx7).

37 Joseph A. Wulfsohn, "From 'smear campaign' to 'Russian disinformation,' liberal media teamed up to dismiss Hunter Biden story," Fox News, December 11, 2020 (https://tinyurl.com/4arnxz3r).

38 *Ibid.*

39 Natasha Bertrand, "Hunter Biden story is Russian disinfo, dozens of former intel officials say," *Politico*, October 19, 2020 (https://tinyurl.com/yza5y5vu).

40 *Ibid.*

41 Kevin Johnson, "DNI Ratcliffe: Russia disinformation not behind published emails targeting Biden; FBI reviewing," *USA Today*, updated October 20, 2020 (https://tinyurl.com/nt7w3hfy).

42 Bruce Golding, "How tweet it is: Twitter backs down, unlocks Post's account," *New York Post*, October 30, 2020 (https://tinyurl.com/2bkp2euk).

43 Kayleigh McEnany, Twitter, October 15, 2020 (https://tinyurl.com/9rj4tmxu).

44 Brooke Singman, "Hunter Biden 'tax affairs' under federal investigation; links to China funds emerge, sources say," Fox News, December 9, 2020 (https://tinyurl.com/5xz9s2vj).

45 Jerry Dunleavy, "Hunter Biden admits laptop 'certainly' 'could be' his," *Washington Examiner*, April 2, 2021 (https://tinyurl.com/4wz3n75t).

46 Lindsey Ellefson, "Washington Post Now Says Trump Never Told Georgia Official to 'Find the Fraud,'" *The Wrap*, March 15, 2021 (https://tinyurl.com/r7uv3x5e).

Chapter 7

1 "Aisne-Marne American Cemetery," American Battle Monuments Commission, (https://tinyurl.com/4fhwwwta).

2 Rob Crilly, "White House officials deny Trump disparaged war dead and say he was 'livid' he could not visit French cemetery," *Washington Examiner*, September 3, 2020 (https://tinyurl.com/vvxy94a).

3 Jeffrey Goldberg, "Trump: Americans Who Died in War Are 'Losers' and 'Suckers,'" *The Atlantic*, September 3, 2020 (https://tinyurl.com/hsk36thc).

4 Rob Crilly, "White House officials deny Trump disparaged war dead and say he was 'livid' he could not visit French cemetery."

5 "Press Briefing by Ambassador O'Brien, Ambassador Grenell, Senior Advisor Kushner, and Press Secretary Kayleigh McEnany | September 4, 2020, The White House, September 4, 2020 (https://tinyurl.com/57j6r89k).

6 "Press Briefing by Press Secretary Kayleigh McEnany | September 9, 2020," The White House, September 9, 2020 (https://tinyurl.com/usur8kz9).

7 Mark Moore, "Trump points to John Kelly aide who says he never heard 'losers' remarks,'" New York Post, September 7, 2020 (https://tinyurl.com/3janhw8p).

8 Kaelan Deese, "John Bolton says he didn't hear Trump insult fallen soldiers in France," The Hill, September 4, 2020 (https://tinyurl.com/yc26x9bw).

9 Jeffrey Goldberg, "Yes, Yes, I Know I Started the Iraq War," The Atlantic, June 25, 2010 (https://tinyurl.com/y4f3tsvp).

10 Zeke Miller and Alexandra Jaffe, "Biden slams Trump over alleged comments mocking US war dead," Associated Press, September 4, 2020 (https://tinyurl.com/29b6jhkp).

11 John Verhovek, "Biden hammers Trump over alleged 'losers, suckers' comments, targets veterans, Latinos in new slate of ads," ABC News, October 9, 2020 (https://tinyurl.com/tef345zp).

12 Alison Durkee, "Military Households Still Back Trump Over Biden, Despite Bombshell Atlantic Report: Poll," Forbes, September 10, 2020 (https://tinyurl.com/4jh5pxeu).

13 "First American Dies of Coronavirus, Raising Questions About U.S. Response," New York Times, February 8, 2020 (https://tinyurl.com/h2hdhzj8).

14 "Coronavirus (COVID-19) Deaths," Our World In Data (https://tinyurl.com/nsady3w). Chapter 5.

Chapter 8

1 Jonathan Turley, "Written Statement," December 4, 2019 (https://tinyurl.com/ycj49rpj).

2 Fernanda Echavarri, "The President May Have Been the Last Person in America to Find Out About RBG's Death," Mother Jones, September 18, 2020 (https://tinyurl.com/5brzz7zv).

3 "Remarks by President Trump Announcing His Nominee for Associate Justice of the Supreme Court of the United States," The White House, September 26, 2020 (https://tinyurl.com/4dp24ytk).

4 "Franklin Graham Easter 4 12 20," YouTube, April 12, 2020 (https://tinyurl.com/2mj4krdy).

5 Dartunorro Clark, "Fauci calls Amy Coney Barrett ceremony in Rose Garden 'superspreader event,'" NBC News, October 9, 2020 (https://tinyurl.com/ues39fu2).

Chapter 9

1 Helen Regan, et al., "Coronavirus: latest news from around the world," CNN, October 2, 2020 (https://tinyurl.com/7nctv3j9).
2 John Santucci, Katherine Faulders, and Aaron Katersky, "Trump brother hospitalized in New York: Sources," ABC News, August 14, 2020 (https://tinyurl.com/by2ujkbn).
3 Kayleigh McEnany—@PressSec45, Twitter, October 2, 2020 (https://tinyurl.com/duhyz48w).
4 "Explained: COVID-19 PCR Testing and Cycle Thresholds," Public Health Ontario, February 17, 2021 (https://tinyurl.com/vvs6kktm).
5 "Do It Again," Elevation Worship (https://tinyurl.com/6scbpa5p).
6 "New Wine," Hillsong Worship (https://tinyurl.com/3y6k2hy7).
7 Kayleigh McEnany, *The New American Revolution.*

Chapter 10

1 "When You Can be Around Others After You Had or Likely Had COVID-19," CDC, July 16, 2021 (https://tinyurl.com/25vsv6j5).
2 Gabby Orr, "'A huge misstep': Trump allies see a lost opportunity in first debate," Politico, September 30, 2020 (https://tinyurl.com/498dkh62).
3 Vandana Rambaran, "Trump debate coach Chris Christie says president 'too hot' in Biden showdown," Fox News, September 30, 2020 (https://tinyurl.com/hsdt8a3h).
4 Curt Devine, "307,000 veterans may have died awaiting Veterans Affairs health care, report says," CNN, September 3, 2015 (https://tinyurl.com/33pyjeua).
5 *Ibid.*
6 "Read the full transcript of the first presidential debate," *Concord Monitor,* September 30, 2020 (https://tinyurl.com/yw7snpsp).
7 Brittany De Lea, "FLASHBACK: Biden's chief of staff pick admits Obama admin did everything wrong with H1N1," Fox News, November 11, 2020 (https://tinyurl.com/rz5rsb74).
8 Joseph Wulfsohn, "CNN, broadcast networks ignore Hunter Biden revelations, others downplay Senate report," Fox News, September 24, 2020 (https://tinyurl.com/4ktxxjxf).
9 The Editorial Board, "The Cost of Bidenomics," *Wall Street Journal,* October 18, 2020 (https://tinyurl.com/hupd6jke).
10 The Editorial Board, "The Higher Wages of Growth," *Wall Street Journal,* September 16, 2020 (https://tinyurl.com/2bstz3sn).
11 *Ibid.*
12 Mark Moore, "China continues to block US scientists from examining coronavirus: Pompeo," *New York Post,* April 23, 2020 (https://tinyurl.com/y858d7f6).

13 "Do It Again," Elevation Worship (https://tinyurl.com/6scbpa5p).

14 Matthew 18:20, Bible Gateway (https://tinyurl.com/v9p9uh6u).

15 Kenneth Garger, "Plexiglass removed from debate stage after Trump, Biden test negative for COVID-19," *New York Post*, October 22, 2020 (https://tinyurl.com/fzbcvjsn).

16 "Presidential Debate at Belmont University in Nashville, Tennessee," The Commission on Presidential Debates, October 22, 2020 (https://tinyurl.com/3ztr68vt).

17 Morgan Phillips, "Biden used Russian bounty story against Trump in 2020 campaign," Fox News, April 16, 2020 (https://tinyurl.com/zm2k3a37).

18 Morgan Phillips, "Biden clears way for Russian pipeline after blocking Keystone Pipeline in US," Fox Business, May 18, 2021 (https://tinyurl.com/52xsh7rk); "Psaki Admis Nord Stream 2 'Threatens' Security While Struggling To Justify Biden Lifting Sanctions," YouTube, May 20, 2021 (https://tinyurl.com/c6ej7sax).

19 David Harsanyi, "What does Vladimir Putin have on Joe Biden?" *New York Post*, May 21, 2021 (https://tinyurl.com/37yfkjw5).

20 Noah Manskar, "Jack Dorsey says blocking Post's Hunter Biden story was 'total mistake' – but won't say who made it," *New York Post*, March 25, 2021 (https://tinyurl.com/8hebsa3).

21 Jordan Davidson, "Poll: One In Six Biden Voters Would Have Changed Their Vote If They Had Known About Scandals Suppressed by Media," *The Federalist*, November 24, 2020 (https://tinyurl.com/c3zcwu9c).

22 "Trump and Biden Final Face Off; Candidates Acted Civil and Calm; Both Candidates Scored Points. Aired 10:35-11p ET," CNN, October 22, 2020 (https://tinyurl.com/3rb5x2vd).

23 "CNN's Tapper: 'Biden Struggled When Trump Confronted Him' On His Record," YouTube, October 22, 2020 (https://tinyurl.com/zsh832cr).

24 "ABC's Karl: Trump Successfully Highlighted Biden's Long Record Of Accomplishing Little," YouTube, October 22, 2020 (https://tinyurl.com/9th5te9c).

25 "CBS News' Reid: Trump 'Succeeded' In Highlighting Hunter Biden," YouTube, October 22, 2020 (https://tinyurl.com/4uyzx98c).

Chapter 11

1 Kayleigh McEnany, "Obama tries to demonize Trump voters, following Hillary's losing strategy," Fox News, updated September 10, 2018 (https://tinyurl.com/5k6xembz).

2 "Reps. Meadows, Gaetz, Gowdy, Jordan react to heated Strzok hearing," Fox News, updated July 13, 2018 (https://tinyurl.com/yrm2m7pn).

3 Joseph Wulfsohn, "CNN Don Lemon panel faces intense backlash for mocking Trump supporters as illiterate 'credulous rubes,'" Fox News, January 28, 2020 (https://tinyurl.com/uffrb3vr).

4 Nikolas Lanum, "McEnany rips Biden's 'Neanderthal' remark on 'Fox & Friends,' compares it to Hillary's 'deplorables' insult," Fox News, March 4, 2021 (https://tinyurl.com/7yw7p32p).

5 "Air Force One," The White House (https://tinyurl.com/ree3me8f).

6 Tyler Rogoway, "30 Fascinating Photos of HMX-1's Ospreys Working For The White House," Jalopnik, June 13, 2015 (https://tinyurl.com/sttd55bu).

7 Clare McCarthy, "Kayleigh McEnany tweets footage of 'thousands upon thousands' of Donald Trump supporters lining the streets as his motorcade passed in California," The Daily Mail, October, 19, 2020 (https://tinyurl.com/hc8b6htp).

8 "Travel Pool #9 – Returning to the White House," White House Pool Reports, September 22, 2020 (https://tinyurl.com/v84whuzj).

9 Leviticus 11:10, BibleHub.com (https://tinyurl.com/8h2958jd).

10 Matthew 16:2–3, BibleGateway.com (https://tinyurl.com/re9thm6m).

11 David Jeremiah, "The Jeremiah Study Bible," (https://tinyurl.com/55phjw5s).

12 Matthew 16:2, BibleGateway.com (https://tinyurl.com/dz3c9sr9).

Chapter 12

1 Patrick Whittle & Ellen Knickmeyer, "Trump allows commercial fishing in marine conservation area," *Associated Press*, June 5, 2020 (https://tinyurl.com/btv3utwv).

Chapter 13

1 Nancie Petrucelli, MS, Mary B Daily, MD, PhD, and Tuya Pal, MD, "BRCA1- and BRCA2-Associated Hereditary Breast and Ovarian Cancer," GeneReviews, December 15, 2016 (https://tinyurl.com/22xhz3pd).

2 Kayleigh McEnany, "Why May 1 is the day that will save me from breast cancer forever," Fox News, April 28, 2018 (https://tinyurl.com/ywytnmbw).

3 *Ibid.*

4 Alexis Nedd, "10 Times Dr. K Made Everyone Cry on *This Is Us*," Cosmopolitan, September 11, 2017 (https://tinyurl.com/b32d7yz4).

5 Dave Barnes, "Carry Me Through" (https://tinyurl.com/y43t4z7t).

6 Kayleigh McEnany, "After my 2018 preventive double mastectomy, here's how I'm doing," Fox News, August 26, 2019 (https://tinyurl.com/v3pvre75).

7 Kayleigh McEnany, "Why May 1 is the day that will save me from breast cancer forever."

8 "Transcript: Kayleigh McEnany's RNC remarks," CNN, August 27, 2020 (https://tinyurl.com/jta4bxj8).

9 *Ibid.*

10 "U.S. Breast Cancer Statistics," BreastCancer.org, last modified February 4, 2021 (https://tinyurl.com/y8733y6t).

11 Andrew Erwin & Jon Erwin, "I Still Believe," 2020 (https://tinyurl.com/av66xb7u).

12 *Ibid.*

13 "Jeremy Camp—I Still Believe," YouTube, February 27, 2020 (https://tinyurl.com/5ysxbc5m).

14 Rachel Aviv, "Enter Sandman," Poetry Foundation (https://tinyurl.com/jxt9mnje).